monsoonbooks

TORAJA

T0150031

Nigel Barley was born south of London in 1947. After taking a degree in modern languages at Cambridge, he gained a doctorate in anthropology at Oxford. Barley originally trained as an anthropologist and worked in West Africa, spending time with the Dowayo people of North Cameroon. He survived to move to the Ethnography Department of the British Museum and it was in this connection that he first travelled to Southeast Asia. After forays into Thailand, Malaysia, Singapore, Japan and Burma, Barley settled on Indonesia as his principal research interest and has worked on both the history and contemporary culture of that area.

After escaping from the museum, he is now a writer and broadcaster and divides his time between London and Indonesia.

ALSO BY NIGEL BARLEY

The Innocent Anthropologist
A Plague of Caterpillars
Not a Hazardous Sport
Foreheads of the Dead
The Coast
Smashing Pots
Dancing on the Grave
The Golden Sword
White Rajah
In the Footsteps of Stamford Raffles *
Rogue Raider *
Island of Demons *
The Devil's Garden *
Snow Over Surabaya *

(* published by Monsoon Books)

TORAJA

NIGEL BARLEY

monsoon

monsoonbooks

Published in 2013
by Monsoon Books Ltd
www.monsoonbooks.co.uk

No.1 Duke of Windsor Suite, Burrough Court,
Burrough on the Hill, Leicestershire LE14 2QS, UK

First published as *Not a Hazardous Sport* by Viking in 1988.

This updated edition published in 2017.

ISBN (print): 978-981-4423-46-5
ISBN (ebook): 978-981-4423-47-2

Copyright©Nigel Barley, 1988

The moral right of the author has been asserted.

All rights reserved. No part of this publication may be reproduced,
stored in a retrieval system, or transmitted, in any form or by any
means without the prior written permission of the publisher, nor be
otherwise circulated in any form of binding or cover other than that in
which it is published and without a similar condition being imposed on
the subsequent purchaser.

Cover design by Cover Kitchen.
Inside page photographs©Nigel Barley.

A Cataloguing-in-Publication data record is available from the National
Library of Singapore.

Printed in Great Britain by Clays Ltd, St Ives plc
20 19 18 17   4 5 6 7

To Din

PREFACE

Traditionally, anthropologists have written about other peoples in the form of academic monographs. The authors of these somewhat sere and austere volumes are omniscient and Olympian in their vision. Not only do they have a faculty of shrewd cultural insight superior to that of the 'natives' themselves, but they never make mistakes and they are never deceived by themselves or others. On the maps of alien culture they offer, there are no dead ends. They have no emotional existence. They are never excited or depressed. Above all, they never like or dislike the people they are studying.

This is not such a monograph. It deals with first attempts to get to grips with a 'new' people – indeed a whole 'new' continent. It documents false trails and linguistic incompetences, refuted preconceptions and the deceptions practised by self and others. Above all, it trades not in generalizations, but encounters with individuals.

From the strict anthropological perspective, these encounters are vitiated by the fact that they took place not in the first local tongue of the people but in Indonesian. The Republic of Indonesia has many hundreds, if not thousands, of local languages. First approaches are therefore always through the medium of the national language, and its use is a mark of the preliminary nature of the contact involved. Such contacts – over the more than two years dealt with by this book – nevertheless turned into relationships of real personal and emotional content.

Monographs are written in reverse. They impose a spurious order on reality where everything fits. This book was written in the course of the experience it documents. A quite different work could have been constructed starting from the magnificent Torajan rice-barn that now stands in the galleries of the Museum of Mankind in London, showing how the plan to build it made ethnographic, financial and museological sense. But that is not the way it happened.

Many people helped in the project that is the matter of this book. In England, the Director and Trustees of the British Museum had the vision to finance such a speculative enterprise. Without the unflagging support and understanding of Jean Rankine and Malcolm McLeod, it could have never come to pass.

In Indonesia, thanks are due to Ibu Hariyati Soebadio of the Departemen Pendidikan dan Kebudayaan, Bapak Yoop Ave and Luther Barrung of the Departemen Parpostel – all of whom led me by the hand through the official channels that I could never have navigated without their continued good will. Bapak Yakob, Bupati of Tana Toraja, Bapak Patandianan of Sospol and Nico Pasaka were ever helpful. In Mamasa, *Drs* Silas Tarrupadang is owed warm thanks for his unstinting hospitality and assistance. Professor and Ibu Abbas of Hasanuddin University went out of their way to help me in a time of dire need. One *anti*-acknowledgement is due to Bapak W. Arlen of the Immigration Office, Ujung Pandang.

I am also grateful to H. E. Bapak Suhartoyo and Bapak Hidayat of the Indonesian Embassy in London. A special vote of thanks is due to Bapak W. Miftach, also of the Indonesian Embassy in London, for his sustained support, assistance and friendship throughout this project.

The Torajan Foundation of Jakarta – especially Bapak J. Parapak and Bapak H. Parinding – took a warm personal interest in the Torajan exhibition from its inception and acted as sponsors, as did Garuda Indonesia.

Without the cheerful friendship, assistance and understanding of Sallehuddin bin Hajji Abdullah Sani, this project would not have been conceived and could not have been executed.

Above all, thanks are due to the many ordinary Torajan men and women who took me to their hearts and aided me without thought of reward or personal convenience.

Nigel Barley

NEW DEPARTURES

'Anthropology is not a hazardous sport.' I had always suspected that this was so but it was comforting to have it confirmed in black and white by a reputable insurance company of enduring probity. They, after all, should know such things.

The declaration was the end result of an extended correspondence conducted more in the spirit of detached concern than serious enquiry. I had insured my health for a two-month field-trip and been unwise enough to read the small print. This being the 1980s and the world as it was, I was not covered for nuclear attack or nationalization by a foreign government. Even more alarming, I *was* covered for up to twelve months if hijacked. Free-fall parachute jumping was specifically forbidden together with 'all other hazardous sports'. But it was now official: 'Anthropology is not a hazardous sport.'

The equipment laid out on the bed seemed to contest the assertion. I had water-purifying tablets, remedies against two sorts of malaria, athlete's foot, suppurating ulcers and eyelids, amoebic dysentery, hay fever, sunburn, infestation by lice and ticks, seasickness and compulsive vomiting. Only much, much later would I realize that I had forgotten the aspirins.

It was to be a stern rather than an easy trip, a last pitting of a visibly sagging frame against severe geography where everything would probably have to be carried up mountains and across ravines, a last act of physical optimism before admitting that urban life and middle age had ravaged beyond recall.

In one corner stood the new rucksack, gleaming iridescent green like the carapace of a tropical beetle. New boots glowed comfortingly beside it, exuding a promise of dry strength. Cameras had been cleaned and recalibrated. All the minor tasks had been dealt with just as a soldier cleans and oils his rifle before going into battle. Now, in pre-departure gloom, the wits were dulled, the senses muted. It was the moment for sitting on the luggage and feeling empty depression.

I have never really understood what it is that drives anthropologists off into the field. Possibly it is simply the triumph of sheer nosiness over reasonable caution, the fallibility of the human memory that denies the recollection of how uncomfortable and tedious much of field-work can be. Possibly it is the boredom of urban life, the stultifying effect of regular existence. Often departure is triggered by relatively minor occurrences that give a new slant on normal routine. I once felt tempted when a turgid report entitled 'Applications of the Computer to Anthropology' arrived on my desk at the precise moment I had spent forty minutes rewinding a typewriter ribbon by hand because my machine was so old that appropriate ribbons were no longer commercially available.

The point is that field-work is often an attempt by the researcher to resolve his own, very personal problems, rather than an attempt to understand other cultures. Within the profession, it is often viewed as a panacea for all ills. Broken marriage? Go and do some field-work to get back a sense of perspective. Depressed about lack of promotion? Field-work will give you something else to worry about.

But whatever the cause, ethnographers all recognize the call of the wild with the certainty that Muslims feel about the sudden, urgent need to go to Mecca.

Where to go? This time, not West Africa but somewhere fresh. Often I had been asked by students for advice on where to go for field-work. Some were driven by a relentless incubus to work on one topic alone, female circumcision or black-smithing. They were the easy ones to counsel. Others had quite simply fallen in love with a particular part of the world. They, too, were easy. Such a love affair can be as good a basis for withstanding the many trials and disappointments of ethnography as any more stern theoretical obsession. Then there was the third, most difficult group, into which I myself seemed now to fall – what a colleague had unkindly termed the Social Democratic Party of anthropology – those who knew more clearly what they wanted to avoid than what they wished to seek.

When advising such as these, I had always asked something like: 'Why don't you go somewhere where the inhabitants are beautiful, friendly, where you would like the food and there are nice flowers?' Often such people came back with excellent theses. Now I had to apply it to myself. West Africa was clearly excluded, but the answer came in a flash – Indonesia. I would have to make further enquiries.

I consulted an eminent Indonesianist – Dutch, of course, and therefore more English than the English with his houndstooth jacket, long, elegant vowels and a Sherlock Holmes pipe. He pointed the stem of it at me.

'You are suffering from mental menopause,' he said, puffing roundly. 'You need a complete change. Anthropologists always go to their first field-work site and make the hard discovery that people there are not like the people at home – in your case that the Dowayos are not like the English. But they never get it clear that *all* peoples are unlike each other. You will go around for years looking at everyone as if they were Dowayos.

13

Do you have a grant?'

'Not yet. But I can probably sort out some funding.' (The saddest thing about academic research is that when you are young you have plenty of time but no one will give you any money. By the time you have worked a little way up the hierarchy, you can normally persuade someone to fund you but you never have enough time to do anything important.)

'Grants are wonderful things. I have often thought that I would write a book about the gap between what grants are given for and what they are actually spent on. My car,' – he gestured through the window – 'that is the grant to get my last book retyped. I sat up all night for six weeks and did it myself. It is not a very good car, but then it was not a very good book. I got married with a grant to enable me to study Achinese. My first daughter has a grant to allow me to visit Indonesian research facilities in Germany.' Academics. The culture of genteel poverty.

'You got divorced recently. Did you get a grant for that?'

'No … That one, I paid for. But it was worth it.'

'So where should I go?'

He puffed. 'You will go to Sulawesi. If anyone asks why, you will explain it is because the children have pointed ears.'

'Pointed ears? Like Mr Spock?'

'Just so. We have him too.'

'But why?'

He puffed smoke like an Indonesian volcano and smiled mysteriously. 'Just go and you will see.'

I knew I was hooked. I would go to the island of Sulawesi, Indonesia, and look at the pointed ears of the children.

There may be pleasure in the remote anticipation of a journey. There is none in its immediate preparation. Injections. Should one really believe that smallpox has been 'eradicated'? – a nice, clean, hard-edged word that was infinitely suspicious.

Rabies? How likely were you to be bitten by a rabid dog? Yes, but you can catch it by being scratched by a cat or pecked by a bird. Gammaglobulin? The Americans swear by it. The British don't believe in it. Ultimately, you make an arbitrary choice like a child grabbing a handful of sweets. How many shirts? How many pairs of socks? You never have enough to wear but always too many to carry. Cooking pots? Sleeping bags? There will be moments where both will be indispensable but are they worth the suffering involved in carrying them across Java? A review of teeth and feet, treating one's body like a troublesome commodity in a slave market. A time to look at guidebooks and the previous works of ethnography.

Each seemed to tell a different story. Planning a route was impossible. They could not be reconciled into a unified vision. According to one, Indonesian ships were floating hell-holes, the nadir of degradation, filthy and pestilential. Another viewed them as havens of tranquillity. One traveller claimed that he had travelled tarmac roads which another traveller declared to have been cancelled. Travel books were as much works of fantasy as grant applications. My Dutchman probably wrote them. A secondary problem was that you could never be sure of the values of the writer. One man's 'comfortable' was another's 'absurdly expensive'. In the end, the only thing to do was go and look.

There is a stage at which maps appear essential. In fact, they merely give a spurious sense of certainty that you know where you are going.

Map men are the true eccentrics of the book trade – wild-haired, glasses-pushed-up-on-forehead sort of people.

'A map of Sulawesi? Charlie, we've got one here wants a map of Sulawesi.' Charlie peered over a stack of maps at me. Apparently, they didn't get the Sulawesi type here every day. Charlie was the glasses-pushed-down-to-tip-of-nose sort.

'Can't do you one. We'd love one for ourselves. Do you a pre-war Dutch one with nothing on it. Indonesians have the copyright you see. Frightened of spies. Or you can have an American Airforce Survey but it comes on three sheets six foot square. Lovely bit of cartography.'

'I'd hoped for something a little more convenient.'

'We can do you East Malaysia Political. You get the rest of Borneo Physical Features up the far end and four inches of South Sulawesi to make up the square. But I suppose if you want to go more than ten miles from the capital, that's not much use. We can do you a street map of the capital with directory.'

I looked at it. How often had one studied these ambitious tangles of streets and avenues that resolved themselves on the ground into hot, dusty little villages with only one real road.

'No. I don't think so. Anyway, the name's changed. It's not called Macassar any more. It's Ujung Pandang.'

Charlie looked shocked. 'My dear sir. This is a 1944 map.' It was too. The directory was in Dutch.

Money being, as ever, in short supply, it was time to phone around the bucket-shops for a cheap ticket. One could not reasonably hope to find one to Sulawesi. The best thing would be to get to Singapore and hunt around.

What is astonishing is not that fares should vary from one airline to another, but that it is virtually impossible to pay the same fare to fly by the same airline on the same plane. As the trail cleared and the prices declined, the names of airlines seemed less and less real and more and more revealing. Finnair suggested a vanishing trick. Madair was expensive but suggested a bout of wild adventure. In the end, I settled for a Third World airline described as 'all right once you're in the air'. In an attic above Oxford Street, I rendezvoused with a nervy little man who looked like a demonstration of the disastrous effects of stress – wizened, twitchy, biting nails, chain-smoking. He was surrounded with huge heaps of paper and a telephone that rang incessantly. I paid my money and he began writing out the ticket. Ring, ring.

'Hallo. What? Who? Oh dear. Ah, yes, well. I'm sorry about that. The problem is that at this time of the year all the traffic is going East so there *will* be a problem in getting a seat.' There followed five minutes of placatory explanation to someone on the other end of the line who was manifestly very annoyed. He hung up, bit his nails and returned to writing out the ticket. Immediately, the phone rang again.

'Hallo. What? When? Oh dear. Ah, well. The problem is that at this time of year all the Asians are heading West so there will be problems getting a seat.' Another five minutes of soothing noises. He sucked desperately on a cigarette. Ring, ring.

'Hallo. What? Oh dear. I am sorry. That's never happened before in all the years I've been in this business. I certainly posted the ticket to you.' He picked through a wad of tickets, put one in an envelope and began scribbling an address.

'The trouble is that at this time of year, most of the Post Office is on holiday, so there will be delays.'

It was with the direst forebodings that I pocketed my ticket and left the office.

And so I arrived at pre-departure depression. Having taken a turn about the room with the beetle-carapace rucksack, I unpacked it and threw half the contents out. I needn't have bothered. When I arrived at the airport, there was no room on the plane and no other plane for a week. I rang the pre-stressed travel agent.

'What? Who? Well, that's never happened before in all the years I've been in the business. The problem is that at this time of year the extra planes are held up by the monsoon. But I'll give you a full refund. I'm putting it in an envelope now.' When the cheque arrived, several weeks later, it bounced.

It is said that every positive term needs its negative to sharpen its definition and fix its place in the wider system of things. This is perhaps the role of Aeroflot in the airline world – a sort of antithetical airline. Instead of effete stewards, burly moustachioed wardresses. Instead of the fussy congelations of aircraft cuisine, fried chicken. Between London and Singapore, we ate fried chicken five times, sometimes hot, sometimes cold, always recognizable. Rather than lug my luggage back home, I had opted for the only cheap flight that day – on Aeroflot.

Some strange smell like oil of cloves had been introduced into the air supply. It was particularly pungent in the lavatory – a place entirely devoid of paper – and as a result of it, people would emerge red-faced and gasping. At moments of stress, such as landing, cold air streamed visibly from vents in the ceiling as off dry ice in a theatrical production. This terrified the Japanese who thought it was fire and whimpered until a wardress shouted at them in Russian. Thereafter they were not convinced but at least cowed.

The only relief from the bouts of fried chicken was the changing of planes in Moscow. Emerging in late evening from the miasma of cloves, we were made to queue on the stairs under 20 W bulbs as in a municipal brothel. Wardresses rushed among us inquisitorially shouting 'Lusaka!' Or was it 'Osaka!'? Japanese and Zambians jostled each other without conviction. Our tickets were minutely examined. Our luggage was searched. A scowling young man checked our passports, reading them line by line with moving lips. He insisted on the removal of hats and glasses. Myself, he measured to check my actual height against that alleged in my passport. I cannot believe that the figures matched.

The girl behind me was French and garrulous, eager to tell her life-story. She was going to Australia to get married. 'I expect it will be all right when I get there,' she said gamely. Having a well-developed sense of humour, she found my being measured exquisitely funny. 'They measure you for a coffin?' she suggested cheerfully. The scowling young man did not appreciate her levity and sent her to the back of the queue to stand in line again. It was just like being back at school. In fact the whole transit area recalled drab, post-war school-days. Stern ladies wheeled trolleys of chipped cream enamel, meaty faces set in disapproval. Surely these were the very women who had dispensed fatty mince at my primary school while discussing the problems of rationing. The broken lavatories of the airport recalled the outhouses of the school.

Younger women in olive-green uniforms saluted soldiers sauntering about with rifles. They had the air of those on important state business. An air of guilt and insecurity seemed to invade the Westerners. We all felt improperly frivolous and facetious, like gigglers at a funeral. One day, perhaps, we would grow up into sober citizens like these people.

All the shops were shut, thus preventing us rushing in to buy nests of Russian dolls and books on Vietnamese collectivization. More adventurous souls discovered a bar upstairs where fizzy mineral water could be bought from a dour man with no change.

We had all been issued with squares of cardboard on which someone had written 'diner 9.00'. There was an area of tables and chairs so here we all sat down looking more and more like refugees. At ten o'clock the school-dinner-ladies emerged, adjusting their headscarves for action. But, alas, there was no mince for us. They served a copious and leisurely meal to themselves, consumed before our envious eyes with great lip-smacking gestures of content. For once, no chicken seemed to be involved. The ladies disappeared and went into a prolonged bout of off-stage plate-clattering. Shortly before our plane was due to leave, they surged out triumphantly with the enamel trolleys. One served us two slices of bread, a tomato and black coffee while two others shooed us into tight groups and examined tickets. When all expectation of more had been abandoned, we were served a single biscuit on magnificent china.

Beneath us, in the space before the departure gates, a lively floor-show was in progress. Two tourists, English by the sound of them, were banging on the glass door of the immigration office. They had tried pushing it. They had tried pulling it. They did not know it was a sliding door.

'Our plane!' they shouted, indicating what was indeed a large aircraft parked just the other side of the plate-glass window. Passengers could be seen embarking. A rotund official in a sackcloth uniform stared out of the window, his back turned towards them, and worked hard at ignoring the noise they were making.

'You phoned us to come to the airport,' they cried. 'We've been waiting a week for a plane.'

Finally, the disturbance grated on his nerves and, unwillingly, he slid the door open an inch to peer at them like a householder wakened by knocking in the small hours. They thrust tickets at him in justification. This was a mistake. He took them, peacefully closed and locked the door, set the tickets on the end of his desk and resumed his untroubled contemplation of the plane. A wardress appeared at the top of the steps, looked briefly around, shrugged and went back inside.

'Call someone,' the travellers pleaded. 'Our luggage is on that plane.'

In response, the official deftly slid the tickets back under the door and turned his back again. The hatch of the plane was closed, the steps wheeled away. The travellers began hammering on the door in renewed desperation. The official began to smoke. We watched for a full ten minutes before the plane finally roused itself to trundle off. By then, the travellers were sobbing.

Pharisaically, we turned away. Our own plane had finally been called. Following this little morality play, no one wanted to be late. We bayed around the doors like pagan hordes at the gates of Rome. Occasionally, a wardress would appear behind the glass doors and we would surge forward. Then she would disappear again and leave us stranded in foolishness.

The resumed flight brought no relief, only more fried chicken. A bumptious Indian paced the plane, telling all and sundry that he was an admiral in the navy and only travelled by Aeroflot for security reasons, not out of parsimony. In one corner sat a Seasoned Traveller. She dismissed all offers of chicken with a disdainful wave of the hand, having had the foresight to provision herself with a selection of cheeses and a good loaf. At her feet stood a bottle of wine. On her lap rested a stout novel. Most outrageous of all, she had soap and a toilet roll. We regarded her with the undisguised resentment of those faces at the windows of old folks' homes. We took pleasure in the fact that, as we began our descent to Singapore, a green-faced man emerged from the lavatory and kicked her wine over.

Singapore. The Lion City. Its current symbol – current because everything in Singapore is subject to a ruthless process of revision and improvement – is the merlion, a sickly, coy confection of lion and fish worthy of Walt Disney. Down by the harbour, it belched a spume of dirty water for the sole purpose of being photographed doing so by tourists.

After Moscow it was unmistakably part of the free world but also a place of control and order. The city state's social charter invokes the name of Raffles, commemorated in place-names all over the island. But its founder, saviour and benevolent despot, Lee Kuan Yew, goes uncommemorated. It is a republic and Lee Kuan Yew is its king. British names have been retained everywhere.

To visit the air base is a joy. Bland Chinese officers sit outside bungalows called 'Dunroamin', on roads called 'The Strand' and 'Oxford Street'. Singapore has felt no need to obliterate its colonial past. Like everything else, it has been smoothly absorbed.

If Lee Kuan Yew's name is not omnipresent, his personality imbues all levels of the state. You may not cross a road except at a traffic light (fine $500), or spit (fine $500), or drop litter (fine $500). It is believed that all problems can be solved by making more rules. Again, as in Moscow, the school is the analogy by which we understand all authoritarian systems. Not, of course, the breeding grounds of vice, violence and criminality that are modern English schools, but those strangely innocent institutions of the post-war years. Public spaces are neat and well-tended, every scrap of ground becoming a park. In the huge, terrifying tenements, all the lifts work and are spotlessly clean. Singaporeans, mysteriously, do not bemerde their own surroundings. Even public telephones work. It is a shocking contrast to the squalid self-mutilation of urban London.

It is above all a city dedicated to earning a living. Many have praised the industriousness of Singaporeans. But it is a curious form of industry that seems to consist largely of traders sitting in shopping centres, surrounded by goods made in Japan and sold largely to Westerners. Even by British standards the rudeness of salesmen is astonishing, despite a personal 'Smile' campaign by Lee Kuan Yew. (Again one thinks of the school – the headmaster rising to his feet in assembly, 'I should like to say a few words about the general lack of cheerfulness in the school.') The English spoken is extraordinary. In this polyglot mix of Chinese, Indians and Malays, some people seem to have ended up with no first language at all.

I stayed with a Malay family in one of the high-rise blocks of steel and concrete that have replaced the old, friendly wooden shacks in which Malays once lived in insanitary ease. By conscious policy, the races are mixed. On one side Indians, on the other Chinese. The corridors are awash with the odours of contesting spices and incense sticks for various gods. Different tongues quack and growl in the stairwells. Inside, five adults and two children dwelt in three small rooms and a kitchen, all spotlessly clean. Stay in a hotel? Nonsense. There is room here. You are as one of our family.

Malay hospitality is overwhelming. The only burden is the obligation to eat three times, as much as you would wish.

It was my first opportunity to try out the Indonesian language – almost. Malay and Indonesian are in the same sort of relationship as English and American. The television picked up both Singapore and Malay broadcasts from across the causeway that divides the two states. On the Singaporean channel, only good news. Bad events were a truly foreign phenomenon. Singaporeans were shown in a harmony of multi-ethnic progress. See – the new underground. Behold – more land is being reclaimed from the sea. On the Malaysian channel a darker, handsomer people were demonstrating Muslim virtue. The foreign news was of Mecca and new mosques. 'Are you sure these are not Israeli oranges?' someone asked behind me.

Telephone calls within the city are free. In ten minutes my air ticket to Jakarta had been fixed at a third of the price I would pay in London. I began to feel like a bumpkin.

We settled back to watch a Malay melodrama that seemed to consist of scandalously obvious wives cuckolding their virtuous husbands who were away at the court. The adulterous act was signified by the closing of the bedroom door.

'Listen how she laughs, that one. She is not a virgin.'

'Look. Now she smokes. Wah!'

Sadly, I was unable to understand a word of the film but the anthropologist is schooled from a tender age to sit through dull seminars, boring conferences, incomprehensible presentations. Patience was rewarded. After the infliction of many wrongs on her poor husband, the wife's crimes were denounced by the rajah. The court spoke a dialect close enough to Indonesian to be intelligible. The enormity of her crime at last was revealed. She had stolen the rice given her for her stepchildren and sold it to buy perfume. Wah!

The commercial centre of Singapore is clearly where Westerners go to get away from Asia. It is a place for getting things done. It is full of oil-men, accountants, lawyers and other shady professions in a setting that apes the worst of *Dallas*. The somewhat puritanical government is engaged in waging a baffled war on the tastes of Western tourists, seeming unable to understand that if you remove squalor, irrational practices and all that is called 'local colour', tourists feel that they might as well have stayed at home.

The current preoccupation was Bugis Street, a name to make many an old British sailor's loins tremble. It was famous, quite simply, for its transvestite prostitutes. Transvestism is one of the great themes of the East, often a very serious matter indeed, sometimes with religious implications.

In Bugis Street, however, it was purely for rest and recreation. The government, shocked by 'outrageous exhibitionism' and always solicitous of its image abroad, had decided to close it down. Much was made of this in the newspapers.

'Where is it?' I asked the sons of the house, young men in their twenties. Is it fun to go there?' They held a whispered conversation.

'We do not know where it is. We have never been.'

'Have you a map?'

'We have no map. But I will ask a friend.'

They dragged the telephone off into the bedroom on its long lead and made a call. They made three calls, blushing the while.

'None of my friends know. They are all Muslims.'

'Have you any Chinese friends?'

'I will try.'

Ten minutes later, we were on our way, giggling with conspiracy. We had explained to the father that we were going to look at the lights of the harbour. When we finally found it, Bugis Street was a dark, narrow street of buildings ripe for demolition. Notwithstanding its narrowness, tables and chairs had been set out on the tarmac and a hundred stalls were cooking all manner of food under the stars. Great herds of tourists roamed up and down in search of the thrill of scandal, many taking to eating in despair of other sensual pleasures. I paid for three of the most expensive drinks I have ever had anywhere. A small girl of about five or six was going from table to table, challenging the tourists to noughts and crosses for a stake of $ I. She was doing very well. Immaculate Malay policemen patrolled up and down, disapproval heavy on their brows.

'Why are all the police here Malay?'

The boys laughed. '*All* police are Malay except for the high officers. The Chinese do not like the Malays to know how to fly aeroplanes or fire big guns, so when we do national service, they put us in the police.'

The tourists were clearly bored. A party of English had found a stray cat and were dedicating their evening to feeding it with fish bought at huge cost. An American suddenly cried, 'Quick Miriam. There's one!' A lone transvestite swivelled and pouted through the tables in a tight leather skirt. Miriam, blue-rinsed and determined, gamely leaped through the throng and hosed the 'girl' up and down with her cine-camera. There was a general snapping and clicking of camera cases and swearing in many European tongues as calculations were made about flash. The transvestite played up splendidly, sticking out tongue and buttocks and swaying away on high heels.

Then doubt set in. It had obviously been a street-walker, but the sex remained unproven.

'Jus' some ole hooker,' opined Miriam.

It would have been a rather sad evening, my Muslim friends disappointed to find that wickedness was not necessarily pleasurable, but it was saved by a hugely wizened Chinese waiter.

'You want other dlink?'

'No thank you. Not at these prices.'

'Psst. You want feelthy picture?'

'What?'

'Feelthy picture. You want?' In a rush, it evoked the heat and dust of imperial service, fresh-faced Tommies disembarking from steamers to the wonders of the East. They would be pictures of belly dancers, or slant-eyed beauties, heavy with silver jewellery and voluptuous promise. He palmed on to the table a plastic folder with pictures in numbered pockets.

Oriental men are not hirsute, but somewhere they had found specimens with an almost Caucasian profligacy of body-hair. They had legs like lavatory brushes, shown to advantage since they were dressed in ladies' swimming costumes. Many held feathers and simpered. There was about them something very sad and a little bit funny, like the pin-ups of our grandparents. It was as if they wanted desperately to be wicked but did not quite know how.

Another police patrol came past, two Malays swinging truncheons. They looked hard at my companions, two fellow Malays, their eyes slid over the book before us. They shook their heads and passed on. My companions looked chastened and ashamed. Once more I was being a bad citizen. It was time to go.

As we left, Miriam reached across.

'If you've finished with those pictures, honey, I've a mind to take a look.'

TALES OF TWO CITIES

Airports are the deceitful but unavoidable purveyors of our first impressions of another part of the world. Travel brochures are deliberately misleading and we expect them to be so. They can be lightly shrugged off as mere confections of images. But airports are *real*. They have the rough-edged feel of true experience.

Singapore airport had been functional and efficient, well-planned and purposeful. It looked as if someone had worked out in advance how much it would cost and it had been paid for on time.

Heathrow is a muddle, a pretentious mess, slow, cumbersome – a ship constantly being rebuilt while at sea. The staff are barely polite and exult in the enjoyment of petty powers. A scene that stays with me over the years is that of an earnest Chinese student being harassed by a snickering immigration official whose Middlesex whine he could not understand.

The new airport at Jakarta was superficially attractive, built like a traditional house, open to the world. The total effect was rather like a Pizza Hut afflicted with gigantism. Soldiers stood around idly in indelicately tight uniforms that seemed to leave them with nothing to do with their hands. If you caught their eye, they blushed and played with their boots. We were directed into two channels, one for those with visas, one for those without. I was without. We were asked in Indonesian, one by one, why we had no visa. Everyone was let in after a ritual hesitation.

'Why no visa?'

'Because at the embassy in London, they said I did not need a visa.' My first sentence in Indonesian to an Indonesian. Would it work? From the outside, a language always looks like an implausible fiction. The official paused, frowned and then broke into a huge grin.

'Very nice,' he said and patted me paternally on the arm. At that moment, I knew Indonesia was going to be all right.

The other side of the barrier was raucous with hot, tired people expressing the ritual outrage of bargaining. I was approached by a stocky man with a scar over one eye, lank, greasy hair and very dirty clothes. An obvious pirate. In fact he was very helpful. We launched into bargaining about the taxi fare. He seemed shocked at the venom of my technique acquired in the sterner school of West Africa.

'Am I not a man like yourself? Do my children not have to eat? Why do you insult me by asking so much, etcetera, etcetera.'

'Oh, all right,' he said, 'The normal fare is fourteen thousand.'

He led me to a tiny ramshackle van that stood uneasily among long limousines. Another large man of suspect appearance climbed in. In West Africa, I would have been most unhappy about this. Two against one. The car stopping in a deserted spot. A knife pulled out in the dark. As usual, I dithered, discouraged by lack of fluency. It is very hard to be determined and incoherent at the same time. Too late. We were off.

My companions conversed in a language of dark consonants and gurgled vowels, that was unintelligible to me. This must be Batawi, the language of Jakarta. We were all introduced to each other in an almost courtly manner, exchanged clove-flavoured cigarettes. Smiles all round. I learned the word for matches. The driver launched into a long tirade that I could not follow, reduced again to dumbness, nodding feigned comprehension. One word kept coming up again and again, *cewek*. It seemed always associated with notions of misfortune. What was it? The government, the price of petrol, some metaphysical term of the Muslim faith? In the end, it seemed that some comment was called for on my part.

'What is *cewek*?' I heard myself ask in the quavering tones of a judge asking for a definition of jazz. They both turned and stared at me.

Cewek? They held hands out at chest level as if grasping melons and sketched sinuous curves in the air. Ah, it must be the slang term for women. I wondered what propositions I had agreed to.

We rocketed along in the dark. Hardboard triumphal arches stood by the roadside. Inscriptions announced forty years of freedom. A glow in the sky declared the city, heralded also by a rich sweet smell compounded of human faeces, woodsmoke, badly refined petrol. Fires twinkled in the blackness, railway trucks, burnt-out lorries, shadowy figures picking through heaps of rubbish, the odd desolate shack. Had I been to Indonesia often? No, my first visit. Then, where had I learned to speak? In London. In London, one could learn? Ah, that was good. Yes. Would English *cewek* like Indonesian men? They would love them. But were they not too small? The best things come in small packages. Wah! That was true. They grinned. Now about this *cewek*. Where would we go? No, no. Tomorrow. I was tired. Just a hotel. Not too dear.

They were unabashed. More cigarettes. Normally I do not smoke but it is a useful way of making contact. We pulled up at a small hotel. There was a shouted exchange. Full up. Try round the corner. There it was full up too. Try the new place up there. We stopped at a nondescript building with bare bulbs shining on fresh cement. It was cheap. Everything looked bare and stark but clean. We climbed the stairs for several floors. The taxi men came too. We scaled a ladder and emerged on the roof. Here was a little wooden hut, a hard bed, a fan. It would do. The taxi men beamed. See, they had brought me to a good place. More cigarettes, handshakes.

The hotel was run by students from Manado, Chinese-looking Christians who had strong but ill-defined links of kinship with the owner. To some, as in the West, the term 'student' was a euphemism for dissolute idling. But not to Piet.

Scarcely had I got through the door, before he came to seek me out. I had made the mistake of describing myself in the register as a teacher.

'I am a student,' he announced with deep pride.

'In what subject?'

'*Filsafat.*' In Indonesian, philosophy is a suety subject. 'I have read Aristotle and Sartre and John Stuart Mill. I will discuss my thesis with you. It is called "The Dilemma of Man in a Post-Existentialist World".'

'Er. Perhaps I should eat first. Where should I go?'

I was directed to another place where young men cooked noodles in a converted garage while taking turns on a typewriter.

'You must forgive us. We are students of journalism but we only have one typewriter.'

They typed and fried and chattered in the fierce heat of Java, using the dialect of their native Borneo. They could understand me but not I them. As a last resort, they typed messages to me in Indonesian.

It was an odd area, extremely warm and human after Singapore. Middle-class and very poor housing stood side by side. Off the roads were alleyways in which seethed the life not of a city but a village. Children were ruthlessly scrubbed, food prepared, a living precariously made. People waved and smiled at a stranger, though such figures were not rare, scared their children by offering to give them to him, laughed at their tears. At all hours of the day and night, lines of naked children were marched off to the municipal bathhouse. A sign proclaimed to a disbelieving world, 'Two children is enough.' Food-sellers wandered about, a mad woman ran through the streets making faces.

At the sides of the road ran or rather stood open sewers, blocked by garbage. When it rained, they would overflow, but it would not rain for many months. Children sailed boats in them. A man came and fished for frogs that he would eat. In the dark, I plunged into one. The students of journalism were appalled. They thrust soap into my hands, cooing words of comfort.

'When you leave, we will see you home or the transvestites will get you. They wait for rich Americans outside the hotel. They are very strong.'

But back at the hotel, it was Piet who was waiting. He waved a photocopied article at me. 'Please, I am having difficulties with Einstein.' He spoke as if Einstein were a recalcitrant child.

'It is this sentence in English: "Space is infinite but not without boundaries." What can it mean?'

We wrestled with it for half an hour. Only then did he reveal that he had a dictionary, kept with the fridge, the telephone and everything else of value, under his bed. On top of it was a constantly rotating mixture of cousins tangled up like pullovers in a Harrods sale. They drifted in. They slept. They drifted out. They emerged scratching at all hours. Only Piet's constant watchfulness prevented the importation of *cewek*.

'If my uncle found women here, he would drive us all out on to the street. Just like that. He is a good man.'

'Yes I can see that.'

Up on the roof there was a slight breeze, welcome in the

deadening heat. But the mosquitoes were already whining at the windows. It was time to batten down the hatches and sleep.

I was woken abruptly at 4.30 a.m. by someone shouting in my ear. A fire? No. Someone was announcing with excitement that it was four-thirty West-Indonesian time. They appeared to be using a loudspeaker.

I bleared through the window. The minaret of a mosque reared up a hundred feet away. The muzzles of twin loudspeakers poked at me menacingly. With a loud crackling another muezzin contested the airspace, then another. By the time prayers started seriously at five o'clock, I was the personal focus of five amplified mosques, each bawling out a different part of the message as if marking me out as in special need of salvation. The whole hut shook with their piety. At the end of prayers, the noise would normally have subsided but this was Friday and the airwaves were given over to stern messages concerning obedience to parents and the holy word.

From the roof, the whole quarter could be seen going determinedly about its business like Londoners in an air raid. Across the street, the manager of a shirt-making sweatshop waved and pointed to his rabbits – a new speculation. Children were already abroad, hunting pigeons and playing football. One, looking like a skinned rabbit himself in a ferocious haircut, was being dragged protesting to the mosque by his father. He grinned up at me.

'Why don't you come too?'

'Maybe tomorrow.'

The man who sold satay was sharpening knives with relish like a mass murderer. It was a scene of ordinary people making a difficult living.

There was a polite coughing behind. It was Piet, still wet from a shower, but clutching a large book. Of course, he was a

Christian and would not be going to the mosque.

'It will be hours before anywhere is open,' he said. 'We can sit down and read my thesis together.'

It was at least an hour before I was felt to have demonstrated enough rapt attention to what turned out to be a work of great learning weighed down with the dead hand of obsessive, scholastic classification. It was hard to know what to say.

'Very thorough.'

Piet was well pleased.

'Don't worry. We will have plenty of time to discuss it again later. This version does not have all the additions.'

At the bottom of the stairs, he had posted a new list of regulations. It appeared that it was no longer allowed to bring loaded rifles into the bedrooms. He had also tried hard to forbid the importation of *cewek* unless evidence of matrimony was produced. However, the slippery English terminology for this difficult area had evaded him. It read, 'It is forbidden to enter women except via their husbands.'

It was a day for visiting museums and making contacts with the academic community. That night I would catch the overnight bus for Surabaya at the eastern end of Java and meet the ship that would take me to Sulawesi.

Everyone I had ever met had spoken of the deft pickpockets of Jakarta. Indonesians, it seemed, almost took a perverse pride in the skill of their thieves, the way that the English do in the sheer nastiness of their football hooligans or the nerve of the Great Train Robbers. As a result of constant warnings, I had purchased a sort of bizarre cummerbund that could contain money and the documents that conferred official existence. I put it on for the first time and sallied forth, bathed in sweat and colonially paunched.

The day was spent in fruitless journeyings around the town, in buses, taxis, on foot and in the three-wheeler *bajai* that is powered by a lawnmower motor in terminal distress. At all official venues, I was treated with enormous deference and required to sign a visitors' book. Should I request to see anyone specific, however, it appeared that he or she had not yet arrived or had already left or was at a meeting. Their return, however, was imminent – but unsure. One lady I had been urged to contact was reported with great firmness to have just left her office. I subsequently discovered that she had been in Australia for two years. I changed tactics and tried phoning people before I arrived. This was the moment to envy those Singapore telephones that clicked and hummed and put you through every time. I joined a queue outside a phone box occupied by a man of gigantic girth who devoted himself to the sort of leisurely gossip that is typical of those in occupation. The sun shone hotly. The traffic roared poisonously. A policeman appeared from an office nearby and grinned at me. I grinned back and wiped my brow in comic overstatement. He nodded at the man in the booth and made mouthing gestures with his hands. I nodded back. He beckoned me over.

'Use my phone,' he invited.

I made several calls and offered to pay but was waved away.

'Happy to meet you. Welcome to Jakarta.'

The first telephone calls in a foreign tongue are a daunting business. Incomprehension threatens the tenuous process of understanding from all directions. If people whisper or shout, have funny accents or talk fast, if they cough or a truck goes past, the whole edifice crashes down. The phone call has special conventions. Almost all over the world, people open a call with 'hallo' or the nearest equivalent permitted by their phonetic system. Often, however, it is not a greeting as in English, but merely a sort of call-sign and you have to immediately go into a proper greeting or be considered rude. When telephones were new and baffling in England and etiquette was still at a formative stage, opinions were divided as to whether a call should begin with 'hallo' or 'ahoy'. Now it is 'hallo' everywhere. But it is disconcerting to be half-way through a call and suddenly realize you have no idea of the conventions for ending one. Should you 'wish to hear someone again'? Should you leave them with a cheery 'till we meet again' when you have never indeed met? My first conversations dragged on infinitely, limping far beyond the point at which they should have been killed off. At last, I learned the word *da*, 'goodbye', 'finished'.

How to address people is difficult. To bring themselves in line with the age of broadcasting, Indonesians have had to invent a new word for 'you' that cuts through all the problems of relative age, status and respect that govern the choice of how to address someone you can actually see. When I tried it on the phone, however, everyone laughed at me.

It was time to sort out my bus ticket. Piet disentangled two of the cousins from the pile and charged them with securing me passage. A new notice announced an increase in the price of the rooms.

'Not for you, however,' said Piet. 'You are a friend.'

One of the many nice things about Indonesians is their inability to cope with abstract, formal relationships. In all but the biggest hotels, it is virtually inevitable that you end up eating in the kitchen, explaining your troubles. In a week, you are a member of the family and their concerns are your concerns. In a culture that traditionally largely lacks family names, first names are the normal form of address and ways of getting round all the 'you/I' problems. It is even awkward talking to someone whose first name you do not know since, when talking to Piet, you tend to say not, 'Are you busy today?' but, 'Is Piet busy today?' Contacts swiftly become soaked in a warm wash of emotion.

In a foreign culture, one rapidly regresses to a childhood

state of dependence. It is shaming not to be able to cross the road unaided. But I just couldn't do it. The problem lay not, as is often the case, with the switch from left to right. Indonesians drive on the left. It is rather that street-crossing techniques are totally different. In England you wait for a gap and then simply cross. In Jakarta, there are no gaps. You step out and enter into negotiation with oncoming drivers. They slow down just enough to let you dash across their path and immediately speed up again afterwards. You know which will let you pass and which will not – at least local people do. For the foreigner, street-crossing is squealing brakes, hair's-breadth escapes and much confusion. The two cousins led me across the heart of the city in serene calm as if there were no traffic at all, pointing out objects of interest on the way.

'Here you may buy ice-cream but it will make you ill. All these statues were put up by Sukarno, the founding father of Indonesian independence. We have dirty names for them all. Here is the department store.'

We entered a stumpy tower block whose top was sheathed in tarpaulin, like a present to some giant child who had lost interest half-way through the unwrapping process. It was staffed almost entirely by schoolchildren in clean uniforms. The shelves displayed goods that had been spread out to fill as much space as possible. The schoolchildren leapt eagerly upon the few customers and lovingly wrapped everything, even pencils. Buying anything involved at least three separate stages. It reminded me of something. Ah yes. Russia!

The cousins were astonished. 'How did you know? It was built for us by the Russians when communists were thought to be a good thing.'

We pressed on and bought a bus ticket from a brisk, efficient woman in a spotless office. It was next to a canal clogged with garbage and sewage. We had to step over a dead cat to gain entry.

The cousins conducted me back, holding my hand across roads. Had I seen the fair of Indonesian products? No. It sounded grim. Then, they would take me.

We trekked off through the dust and traffic smoke to the enormous park. As we passed a police station next to a telephone box, a policeman waved. The cousins were awed.

'He knows you? Why does he make his hands like a mouth?'

The fair was intended to make people realize how many good things were made in Indonesia so that it was unnecessary to import them. To the English, all this has a rather flat, familiar 'Buy British' flavour. Stalls on every side displayed every kind of shoes, rice-steamers, furniture, clove cigarettes. A gallery showed very nasty modern carvings from Irian Jaya under the heading, 'Traditional Indonesian Culture'. Yet people seemed to be having rather more fun than one would have expected from any comparable, pious Western event. Food and drink were being consumed with gusto. A pop festival was in full swing, made more enjoyable by the total failure of the microphones. Wide-eyed children were being hauled around in large wooden trays pulled by tractors. Everywhere, there were models and plans. Indonesians obviously do very good models and plans. A whole fantasy-world of building and development blossomed under perspex cases.

In the streets, young men sold Garuda-bird hats of cardboard and tinsel with dyed feathers of purple and green. I chose an unornamented form. The feathers recalled too closely Bugis Street. The effect was quite striking. Two wings of gold and red spread out over the forehead of the wearer. From the centre, reared the hawkish head of a fierce bird, beak parted for the killing of snakes and other undesirables. A venerable Indonesian gentleman who sported similar headgear rushed up and challenged me to a mock cock-fight. It was all very silly and great fun.

As we walked away, we were accosted by a child, very pretty, almost angelic with melting brown eyes and hedgehog-bristling hair. It displayed perfect dentition and pointed at the hat.

'Give me that hat?' It was hard to refuse. I really had intended it for Piet. The child, however, spoiled its chances. 'Give me money.' Immediately, hearts were hardened. The cousins tutted.

'This is my hat,' I said firmly. 'I have bought it for a friend.' The melting eyes became garnets. The child scowled in concentration and pronounced in perfect English.

'Mister old pig.' It ran off making a gesture that the cousins declined to interpret.

It is very hard to think ill of the beautiful and many Indonesians are very beautiful indeed. The initial problem of working there is the opposite of Africa. There, one has to overcome an initial negative valuation, a culture that seems disagreeable in most essentials. The quality of one's ethnography is assessed by the degree to which one manages to overcome such value judgements – 'cultural prejudice', as they are called. Indonesia, thus far, had presented such a fair face, such warm friendliness that it was hard to look behind that for the blemishes that were surely there. Talking to West Africans is always a struggle. You are aware the whole time that you are fighting for understanding, building a bridge between two worlds, subjecting everything to a secondary interpretation. Indonesians, however, seemed to be 'just people'. Interpretation was still below the level of awareness and therefore not available to inspection – a dangerous situation.

There are some events so embarrassing that even years later they may pop into your mind in a lift, in the street, when you are trying to get to sleep, and make you wince or even groan out loud. Jakarta was the scene of one of these.

Before the bus left, I worked out that I would just have time to go to the theatre. Indonesian television is very bad, possibly the worst in the world. One of the benefits of this is that traditional theatre is still flourishing. In many towns of Java, traditional puppet-plays, music and dance still draw large audiences. I had heard of a *wayang orang* troupe, a form of theatre, based, like the puppet-theatre, upon the ancient Hindu texts but with the parts played by human actors. Piet had urged me to go.

'It is fascinating. Especially good are the women, but they are all played by men. You would never know.'

I took my luggage and went, planning to go straight on to the bus. One of the actors was extremely friendly and invited me backstage to see the others putting on their makeup. They waved a cheery greeting and giggled as they slapped pale skin cream over each other. In one corner was one of the players of female parts, carefully painting his face. *Wayang orang* is extremely demanding physically, the actors imitate the stiff stylized movements of puppets. Some were standing on their heads, others exercising like athletes tuning up. A small orchestra tinkled and crashed off to one side. Eager to be polite, I complimented the female impersonator on the quality of his impersonation. In the security of the all-male changing room, I remarked how particularly convincing the breasts were.

A hush fell upon the room. The actor blushed a furious red.

'That,' said one man quietly, 'is my wife you are talking to.' I stammered excuses and fled to the other side of the stage, vowing to strangle Piet the next time I met him. I felt awful, the worst sort of crass and clumsy Westerner. I could not concentrate on the play and was glad when it was time to go.

The bus was air-conditioned and had tinted glass. On the other side of the glass, the cousins waved a tearful farewell. They had come to see me off. Beside me sat a Frenchman, one of the stern ascetic kind, a believer in reason and the scourge of self-denial. He had come to write a paper on Indonesian clinics. He was very boring.

The glass robbed the colours of all their stridency, reducing them to the tired, grey gloom of a winter's day in England. The coldness of the air reinforced the notion, so that it seemed absurd to look outside and see banana stalls and dust rather than the greasy rain of a European motorway.

We had been presented on entry with a little box containing flavoured milk and a brightly coloured cake of pink, yellow and green. The Frenchman rejected his.

'The colours are surely poisonous.'

The seats were designed for Asian legs and two Westerners entered only with difficulty into the space provided.

There was a time when anthropologists explained virtually everything, from the Russian Revolution to the frequency of divorce, with reference to child-bearing practices. Of course, this style was more popular in America than Britain where it was treated as a typically American unnecessary ingenuity. As a student, I had been encouraged to mock the rage induced by swaddling or the insecurity attributed to harsh toilet training. Somehow, one felt, Indonesians had read all those books and believed them.

From a very early age, children are comforted with a heavy, inert, cylindrical pillow known as a Dutch wife. If children are fractious or fretful, they are draped around such a pillow and encouraged to hug it until they fall asleep. Young men, especially, are expected to snuggle up to such chaste bedfellows until marriage. Presumably, spouses then sleep tightly intertwined as pillow substitutes. The result is that Indonesians with nothing to hug are as pipe-smokers with nothing in their mouths, restless and inattentive. On the streets, one sees them talking, and while talking they embrace lamp-posts, the corners of brick walls, the wings of their cars, each other. They are left with a definite need to hug.

As soon as the bus was under way, passengers began to intertwine and fall asleep. Like the pile of cousins, or a basket of puppies, they wrapped their legs round each other and settled heads on each others' chests. Apparent strangers negotiated licences to hug in the interests of sleep. The Frenchman and I sat stonily apart, watchful lest our knees touch.

It would have been difficult to sleep anyway. The driver set off with a vengeance, holding firmly to the centre of the road, overtaking on blind corners and forcing oncoming traffic off the road. Occasionally, he would meet a kindred spirit, an oncoming truck driver who had adopted a similar policy. They would rush towards each other at breakneck speed and only at the last moment recognize their affinity in a wild and giddy swerve.

A television screen displayed a locally produced film. The audience loved it and a certificate confirmed that it had been adjudged suitable for Muslims. I found it acutely painful, recalling, as it did, recent events.

It was an extraordinary comic tale dealing in the fortunes of a household whose venerable head sheltered numerous servants of low instincts, a bevy of nubile trainee nurses and – inevitably – a transvestite boxer-cum-ladies'-maid. The plot centred on the unassigned pregnancy of one of the female servants with a secondary complication that, through linguistic confusion, it was the transvestite who was generally held to be expecting a child.

A stop for food. The passengers untwined and descended. The food was simple and moderately wholesome but the real urgency was the lavatories. The bus was equipped with its own facilities but these had been barricaded by the minimum five suitcases per person that were stacked in the aisle. Once we were in, we could only leave by some enormous act of communal will.

For a Westerner, public excretion is a complex task, though

involving only basic equipment – a central hole flanked by two skid pads. As in the Soviet Union, there is no paper, but unlike that country, water is conveniently provided. The basic design seems unsympathetic to the trouser-wearer. Indonesians, as might be expected, manage very well but Westerners usually emerge looking as if they have encountered a water-throwing practical joker.

Public urination for the male is equally unhandy, involving major technicalities of modesty and cleanliness. Only the left hand may be used, but only the right hand may enter water for cleansing. I was pleased to note that the Frenchman ended up looking as if he had been hosed down.

The passengers climbed back on board and wrapped themselves around each other again. The Frenchman and I resumed our pose of soldiers at attention. We drove in total darkness through some of the most beautiful scenery in the world.

According to the dictionary, *travel* is etymologically connected to Old French *travail,* 'grief, 'hardship'. It was at Surabaya that language reasserted its hold on reality. I had pictured my stay as a simple matter of stepping from bus to boat and sailing away into the rising sun. It was not to be.

The driver had left an hour late, yet arrived in Surabaya an hour early. We descended into a shadowy dawn, a chill in the air that presaged a blistering hot day. The man at the bus station was welcoming. It was too early to go to the city. I could leave my luggage here. Would I like a shower? Only later did I discover the depth of his kindness. There was a drought in the city. The public water-supply had been discontinued. Water had to be bought expensively from dealers with tankers. Had I known, I would have been less prodigal with the contents of his tank. It was the usual arrangement where a cement room contained a tank of water that you simply poured over your head. Over the radio came a sermon wherein I recognized the words for 'greed' and 'lust'. I had not learnt the other vices yet.

As usual, there was an Indonesian happy to take up the brown man's burden and look after me. He was a gaunt, ascetic man who spoke in whispers. Since I was not a Muslim, perhaps I would like him to take me to a church? Then perhaps I would like to eat? After that he fell silent and it was impossible to coax words from him. We ate in a silence that grew increasingly oppressive. He refused all my attempts to pay and proudly drew out some papers that he laid on the table. They were brochures describing English plastic light switches. He had almost trained as an engineer during the revolution but at that time there was so much politics and so little money. Then the English army had come and destroyed the city and he had ended up as an electrician instead. Japanese switches were cheaper than the English but English were better. The dam was breached. Speech flowed from him in torrents – a craftsman talking about a lifetime in his trade, speaking with pride and involvement. He told me of the problems of domestic wiring in enormous detail and in return wished to hear of this wonder 'central heating'. It was only with difficulty that I disengaged myself. He pursued me into the street. Please, what colours were wires in England? Three pin plugs or two pin, which were better? I embarked in a trishaw and was pedalled off at speed, sweat beginning to tickle around the detachable paunch in the rising heat. He stood in the road and waved his brochures in farewell.

When I tried to catch a bus to the harbour, I was taken in charge by another man, an Ambonese of dark Melanesian appearance – fuzzy hair, a nose of almost Irish meatiness; I immediately started thinking of him as Pak Ambon. I began to feel like a baton in a relay race. The harbour? It was difficult, a place of thieves. He had better come with me.

The shipping office was the closest I had so far come to ethnography as remembered in Africa. It was crowded with shifty-looking characters herded about by police. But these were not police as I had met them till now. They were big, hard-looking men with drawn truncheons and tight mouths, wearing steel helmets stamped with the insignia of the military. They pounced on people demanding papers. For the first time I smelt fear, that heavy scent that hangs around government offices in Africa.

Pak Ambon regarded these happenings dispassionately and spat. 'The real army are all right. But these people …'

In defiance of the office hours prominently displayed, all the ticket-offices were shut. A police sergeant banged on his counter with the truncheon and beckoned me over. I was required to explain my business and show my passport. However, it suddenly seemed that I was not being harassed, as I had imagined, but helped. To my huge embarrassment, I was led through a side door to the office of a man who issued tickets. A few minutes later, I re-emerged sheepishly with a valid ticket. The bad news was that there was no ship to Sulawesi for four days. The crowd regarded me without resentment. Pak Ambon reappeared at my side.

'It would be normal to put a thousand rupiahs in the hand of the sergeant. They don't make enough to live on.'

I folded a note in my hand.

'Thank you very much,' I said. There was the briefest flicker around the sergeant's mouth, but the note disappeared with the speed and grace of a fish darting off into deep water.

'You are welcome.'

I turned to thank Pak Ambon but he was not to be easily dismissed.

'I cannot leave you until I know you are in a proper hotel. You are a fellow Christian.'

It is always slightly shocking to be in a country where

Christianity is regarded as a serious religion and not a mere euphemism for godlessness.

Pak Ambon now revealed himself to have been a sailor in his youth. He did a quick round of the old salts present. A hotel? Clean? Not too dear? Soon we were heading back to town in search of a hotel called the Bamboo Den, a nice oriental name. Apparently, it combined a hotel and a language school. Those who could not pay their bills worked it off in teaching irregular verbs. Preferable to washing dishes any time.

It was a vision of hell. Hot, dirty, full of cockroaches so confident of tenure that they sat on the walls and sneered at passers-by.

Pak Ambon waved us away and embarked on a round of hotels. All were wildly expensive. I did not wish to stay at any of these places but knew that I would not be abandoned until I settled. Pak Ambon offered a solution. There was, he volunteered, a place near where he lived. It was admittedly a little far from the centre, indeed it was on the beach, but simple and clean. The only company would be plain fishermen. It sounded excellent. We embarked on the back of a truck-like bus and rattled off in a cloud of blue smoke.

The more sophisticated passengers alighted one by one and were replaced by toothless crones who hugged baskets of fish and schoolchildren who giggled shyly. Houses gave way to rice-fields and glimpses of sand. Suddenly, there were no other cars, just motorbikes driven by young men – each with a girl riding side-saddle on the back. They waved and grinned as they passed us. As always, I began to construct a vision of the hotel I wanted, a place of noble simplicity, standing on the beach, serving simple food to the crash of waves on golden sand.

The hotel was Indonesian Disneyland, a huge structure of garish colours comprising shooting galleries, roundabouts, large, decaying plaster models of Mickey Mouse and Donald Duck. You could buy ice-cream and popcorn. In the midst of it all lay a Chinese hotel, a chain of stifling-hot boxes. It was clearly designed for casual sex. I may have been the only person to ever rent a room for a whole day. But Pak Ambon and I both knew our assumed burdens of responsibility and gratitude were so great that I would spend the night here. It was not inopportune that a fever had begun to burn behind my eyes. I would have to get to bed at all costs. We parted with vague promises to meet again. In the room an ancient air-conditioner exuded bad breath and dripped water. Comments on the charms of the local women had been written on the mattress in biro. Puzzling over some of the terms, I fell asleep.

I awoke to find a twelve-year-old Melanesian girl standing over me and laughing. A hallucination? Unlikely. I said good morning. 'Good evening,' I was corrected. Then Pak Ambon entered, leading by the hand a small, dark boy and carrying what looked like a collapsible cake-stand.

'I have brought you food. My grandchildren did not believe me when I told them about you, so I have brought them to look.'

They looked. They pulled the hair on my arms, admired my big nose and regretted the pertness of their own snouts. We walked on the glutinous mud that constituted the beach and I was unwise enough to mention that I would look for another place to stay tomorrow. Pak Ambon looked depressed.

'I have failed you. Tomorrow I will come at what time?' I protested in vain. 'I cannot abandon you.'

The next day, we tried my guidebook again. It directed us to a hotel that had been demolished years ago. Pak Ambon decided the time had come for firm action. He questioned a soldier guarding a bank. The soldier hugged his sentry-box and gave us an address. I determined to stay there whatever it was like. Fortunately, it was the place I had been looking for, roomy, cool, cheap. There were smiles all round. Pak Ambon refused to let me buy him lunch. He refused to let me pay his bus fare back to his house.

'You would do the same for me if I were lost in England,' he declared. I felt deeply ashamed.

By now, I had begun to recognize the style of the hotels. The front hall was full of good-natured loungers.

'No. I do not really work here. I come to see my cousin.'

Schoolchildren would drop in on their way to and from school and stare at the television long enough to smoke a cigarette. Everyone smoked, even five-year-olds. At the back, lurked a wizened masseuse. She would seize passers-by and crunch the bones of their hands.

'Yes, I thought so. Wind has got into your joints. You need a massage badly.' I never saw her do any business.

It was a cheerful, slovenly sort of an area with disused railway tracks in the middle of the road. In the morning there was a flower-market. In the evening, they sold children's clothes and plastic buckets. The loungers sat and gossiped. Sometimes they giggled at a huge poster showing a happy Indonesian farmer with a hoe over his shoulder striding towards a better future over the words: 'Transmigration. A better life awaits you in Irian Jaya.' It recalled the Australian immigration posters of my own childhood, depicting a man in an undergraduate gown and swimming trunks clutching a diploma. In Irian Jaya, I will. Were the loungers not tempted?

They rolled their eyes. Here was home. They had friends and family. The natives would kill them. Here was better.

In the evening, men changed into sarongs, much cooler in the baking heat. The loungers were firm that I should buy one. I felt I owed them a laugh.

For the Chinese girls in the shop, it was the funniest thing they had heard for months.

'See. The puttyman *(orang putih)* is buying a sarong.' *Putih* is Indonesian for 'white', so puttyman is something of a mishmash of English and Indonesian, perhaps particularly descriptive for the girls at that moment. They giggled.

The loungers were waiting, bright-eyed. They clapped with joy. We got at least an hour's hysteria out of that sarong, It seemed I did everything wrong. I tried to step into it instead of putting it over my head. It was deliriously short, disclosing hairy shins and boots. The loungers made common cause with me. It was too short for a puttyman. They would make the Chinese take it back. They returned with a longer one in garish shades of orange. I tied it up. It fell down. They tied it for me. It was so tight, I could not sit down. The aged masseuse joined us, together with an old lady from the outer islands on her way to Mecca.

'I shall die on the pilgrimage. I knew Sukarno. My house is worth seventy-five million rupiahs. How much did you pay for that sarong? What? You were robbed.'

Thereafter, she watched the television in silence, chewing areca-nut expressionlessly as, on the screen, a virtually naked puttywoman rotated and writhed to pop music. It was a night of textiles. My sarong. The television picture was fuzzy (*ikat*). A patchwork cat wandered in. As a finale, I tried to go upstairs in my sarong and fell flat on my face. They liked that a lot.

My unreliable guidebook declared that Surabaya had been in the past unjustly neglected by the traveller. It was now a place worthy of more consideration. My guidebook was wrong about that. It is a hot industrial town of cheap modern construction, the old city having been almost totally destroyed by the British at the end of the war. Filling up several days was hard work.

Fortunately, one of the loungers had the solution. We would

go to the zoo. Normally, I am wary of Third World zoos, being tender-hearted to animals in the English way. I have visited African zoos where lions were penned up in tiny cages and it was possible to hire a pointed stick to poke them in the eye so they would roar. Sometimes, the animals get their own back. In another African zoo, the trees in the reptile enclosure had been left so long unlopped that the snakes were able to descend directly from them on to the visitors.

Surabaya zoo was by no means bad. There were many fine animals that entertained strong social relations with their keepers.

The architecture implied an odd classification of beasts. The elephants were deemed to be Muslim and dwelt in a sort of concrete mosque. Giraffes, curiously, were Chinese and lived archly in corrugated iron pagodas. Monkeys were deemed Hindu and paced endlessly up and down on tiny stupas. My guide enjoyed all this immensely.

'There are many people here,' I commented.

'Yes. It is the place for prostitutes.'

Unfortunately, he used the euphemism *kupu-kupu malam,* 'night butterflies', 'moths', so that it was some time before I realized the chief attraction was not the Lepidoptera.

Finest of all were the orang-utans (from the Indonesian for 'forest people'). When their keeper went to see them, they leapt upon him with cries of joy, draped their great arms around him with an almost Indonesian need to hug and were carried off on his motorbike – one on the handlebars, another on the pillion.

We walked back through the market-place where one of the most successful lines was Lady Diana talcum powder, with the inevitable sheepdog fringe on the can.

'There is,' said one of the loungers, 'another Englishman in town. At the university. He teaches English. You must go and see him.'

'Well, I didn't come to Indonesia to see Englishmen.'

'Englishmen do not like each other? How strange.'

'What is his name?'

'Godfrey Butterfield MA.'

Godfrey Butterfield MA lived in a block of flats in a slightly seedy part of the city consisting of old Dutch houses, leprous with damp. With its white stucco and black shutters it seemed to have vaguely Tudor ambitions. Inside were dim lightbulbs, sisal carpeting, signs of economy. A creaking cage of a lift aspired to the fifth floor. Large doors led off a landing. Some stood open to allow air to circulate, but all had an outer door of steel bars as in a jail cell.

A young Chinese appeared, clad only in a sarong. It was the same pattern as my own.

'Haro. I Markus. You come in. You sit down. Godfrey still resting. You like dlink?' It almost seemed as if I was expected. He poured an enormous glass of something and tonic. Ah, not gin, rice-spirit. Further signs of economy. He bustled off to another room and there was the sound of voices. He reappeared and waved his hand like a compere introducing a performer.

Godfrey Butterfield MA was also clad in a sarong. A man in his sixties with sparse grey hair. Ridges of fat cascaded down his chest like terraces of rice-fields on a hillside. Women's breasts wobbled as he walked. He seized the proffered glass of something and tonic, drained it and held it out for a refill.

'Hallo,' he said, without surprise. He had a smoker's voice, hands heavily stained with nicotine. There was a rattle of kitchen equipment offstage. Godfrey deposited his bulk with the practised balance of a man shooting a bag of nutty slag down a manhole and adjusted his sarong modestly.

The sarong was the only modest part of him. He launched into an uninterrupted monologue concerning his many talents, the beneficial effects of the climate to which he attributed his staggeringly good physique, the advantages of right-wing politics. No reply seemed called for. The rattle in the kitchen transformed itself into another Chinese but this time trousered and in glasses.

'Godfley. I think pleasure-cooker blow up in three minute.' The pleasure-cooker must be another sign of economy.

'Right,' said Godfrey briskly, 'so you know where you are, this,' he indicated Markus, 'is number one wife. This,' he motioned towards the young man from the kitchen, 'is number two wife. That's how it is.' He carefully scrutinized me for reaction and found none.

'Let's sit on the balcony.'

So there we were, then, Godfrey Butterfield MA, teacher of English, cast, like many an Oxbridge man before him, on this distant shoal by the wrack-tide of a life of drink and pederasty.

Godfrey Butterfield MA installed himself comfily and began a recitation of the central events of his life. It did not occur to him that there was any other possible subject of conversation. I could tell it was a performance smoothed by much repetition. While talking, he held binoculars up to his eyes and studied the scantily clad workmen who were building a tall block across the road. It seemed that he had a wife, seldom visited, in the south of England who was referred to as 'the old bag'. He had come via the RAF in Singapore.

'All gay in those days. Don't know a single one who wasn't.'

Having been seconded to the Dutch after the war, he had somehow never gone home.

'There goes that man in the red shorts again.' Indeed, a very dark man in red began guiding a hopper full of cement. He grinned and waved to Godfrey.

'Corker!'

Reluctantly, he put away the binoculars and regarded me.

'You,' he said, 'must be a teacher.' It was not meant to be a Compliment. He went off and wrestled with the pleasure-cooker.

Number one departed to a lecture at the university where he was a student. Number two, Nico, favoured me with an account of the many rich and beautiful people who had wanted to sleep with him and been refused, while Godfrey returned and threatened us with the contents of the cooker. Something had gone seriously wrong with the chicken. We ate it as a sort of savoury jam, while Godfrey explained the need for firm government and the benefits of a royal family.

'The longer I live away from England,' he explained, 'the clearer all this becomes to me.'

There would be a tin of Lady Di talcum powder in the bathroom. It was time to make excuses and leave. Godfrey insisted on driving me back. Behind the building was parked an ancient but immaculate Morris Minor, incongruous amid the mysteries of the East. It exhaled a smell of waxed leatherette and Surbiton. As we entered, a young man turned the corner of the building. Godfrey leered outrageously and waggled elephantine buttocks in a gesture designed to be alluring. The young man executed a wide circle around us and looked back in a mixture of horror and disbelief.

'Ah,' said Godfrey Butterfield MA, 'he was interested. You could see that.'

SAILOR WAYS

The ship of the state shipping line was a surprise. It was brand new and immaculate. The passengers were a very mixed bunch. Several puttypersons were immediately obvious, the young ones going steerage class, the older ones first class. It seemed proper for me to plump for the middle way, a six-to-a-cabin arrangement.

The steerage-class passengers dwelt in vast, vinyl-upholstered pits where they slept in cousinly entanglement or watched videos. *Towering Inferno* was the big favourite. Their food was the same as everyone else's except that they were allowed to carry it off and enjoy it anywhere on the ship while we were penned in hot, musty dining-rooms where waiters waged war on those wearing plastic sandals. In our own culture, the tie draws the line between the formal and the casual. In Indonesia, the same distinction is made through footwear.

As we sat through the first of many meals of rice and fish, we were addressed in hushed tones by a waiter.

'There's been a knife fight. One Buginese got killed. Eat quickly. I have *cewek* waiting on the dock.' We bent over our plates in masculine solidarity and gobbled away.

The steerage passengers were a volatile and emotional group. Mostly dark Javanese, they were carrying their entire lives in cardboard boxes and bound for a new life as immigrants in the forests of Irian Jaya. For almost all, two children had not been enough. They sat in gloomy groups watching their native Java, and everything that was familiar, disappear for ever. Old people wept. The young looked frightened but excited, ready for a new life, humming Western tunes, sporting T-shirts with Western slogans they could not understand. I wondered how they would fare in the isolation and boredom of farming settlements. A smiling girl wore a T-shirt which was stamped, 'You're beautiful when you're angry. The rest of the time you look like a pig.' She asked me to translate. I thought it best to leave out the bit about the pig. Such clothes were very fashionable, they agreed, but dangerous. Dangerous? Yes, there had been the case of a young man who discovered he was wearing a T-shirt supporting Israel. There were shocked gasps.

The various puttymen were swiftly adopted by Indonesians who gave them tea, pored ceaselessly over maps offering wildly inaccurate counsel and questioned them endlessly over the West. The crew devoted themselves to table-tennis and races round the ship, giggling, in life-jackets. The passengers were requested to join in.

In the evening, a dance was organized. Most went to enormous lengths to look their best. Among the steerage passengers the cardboard boxes were torn open and plundered of their concealed finery, bright sashes and red shoes. On the upper decks, well-manicured administrators delved into their Gucci luggage for lightweight suits and Dior scarves. Then they all went to the ballroom and sat bolt upright on hard chairs listening to a group of young men singing in pop-pidgin. Everyone was silent and serious as at a classical recital. Children, ramrod-straight, scrubbed, hair gleaming, crossed their arms and behaved like little saints. The singer advanced to the microphone and began a sobbed and gasped version of an English song. It was clear that he did not understand a word of what he had internalized; indeed, he had merely learned certain English sounds that were mixed liberally with gibberish.

'Oh baby. I smug plag pigbum ergle plak. Oh yeah.'

On deck, a full moon was illuminating a seascape of classic beauty. In the bath-warm distance, gallant little fishing vessels bobbed and bucked in glassy isolation as on a corny lacquer tray. Flying fish dived in and out of the spray in our wake, flashing their fins in the moonlight.

I leant on the rail, feeling vaguely poetic. It was a scene for a Noel Coward sentimental encounter, a prelude to shipboard romance. From around a bulkhead appeared an aged puttyman, smoking a George Burns cigar. We looked at each other in mutual embarrassment. He indicated a splodge of light in the sky with the wet butt of the cigar.

'Uranus,' he growled in a whisky voice, 'or maybe Pluto. I not sure.' The accent was heavy Italian. A green glow lay low on the horizon.

'Venus?' I essayed.

'Venus? Si, is possible.' The drone of an aeroplane became audible. Venus began flashing and moved off rapidly towards Java.

'Which way are we heading?'

'We go north ... or maybe south-east. I was in the Italian airforce but I forget.'

A door opened and the pop-singer's voice blew across the ship

'Oh girl. Ee chiliwzdid tagko dud. Oh yeah.'

At sea, the world rises early. A mosque had been established at the rear of the vessel. Many of the faithful, the sophisticates of a world religion, had compasses set into their prayer-mats. More reliable than the Italian airforce, they showed clearly that we were headed due east like all those magic carpets. Infidels such as myself found ourselves stranded at the top of the ship since there was no way back that would not involve wading through the worshippers. Land was close – the territory of true ethnography as opposed to this no man's land of East and West. The first island appeared on one side, houses on stilts clustered away from the seaward side. It looked like heaven but it could be hell to live there. High-prowed Buginese sailing vessels converged like moths around a flame.

A tangle of cranes and derricks were etched against the horizon. Flying fish reappeared about the prow. No, not flying fish – something else. Used condoms, a tribute to the burgeoning Indonesian rubber industry, two children enough. We sloshed towards the harbour. As we entered, a dead dog washed out to meet us, nested on a bed of curled condoms.

Delay, obfuscation. Army officers from the first-class cabins were bowed and scraped about by soldiers carting their chattels and respecting their wives. The emigrants lurked darkly aboard, crouched behind fortified positions of cardboard boxes. Finally stairways clanged against the sides. We had reached Sulawesi.

On the ship, I had found a pulp travel-magazine containing two articles of ethnographic import. The first dealt with an area of Africa where I had previously done field-work. It transformed the local people into a mere fashion accessory, an amusing example of certain extreme forms of self-ornamentation. The second was concerned with Sulawesi and the Toraja. It dealt with the 'explorations' of an intrepid lady reporter. She described herself as 'plunging' into the Toraja area, 'fighting her way' across country and 'pitting herself' against the mountains. From the route described, it was quite clear that she had confined her endeavours to the tarmac roads and probably travelled by bus. This troubled me since I had noticed in myself a tendency to think in the same terms. The West sees it as the duty of the East to be savage but also mysterious. A little brutality is also found to be titillating but should not be of the crude African sort – rather something of exquisite complexity. The lady journalist had met these requirements by including an otherwise totally irrelevant section on Japanese war-crimes in the area. The occupation forces had, it seemed, not merely brutalized the inhabitants but introduced flower-arranging as well. It all looked a little desperate.

The city of Ujung Pandang was clearly not ethnographic territory as such. It was hot, dusty, only marginally cooler than Surabaya.

The best spot in town was obviously the waterfront, where people gathered to sit on the harbour wall and watch the sunset as food stalls were set up on the landward side. Small children came to bathe in the filthy water, wading out some quarter of a mile before it shelved away steeply. Inside an expensive tourist hotel, a sanitized version of the food stalls had been set up at ten times the price. Foreigners could be seen gazing wistfully at the children who seemed to be having all the fun, screaming with joy as they jumped off the piles that supported the hotel over the water. Their favourite sport was taunting a pot-bellied security guard out on to the piles and then leaping joyfully into the sea, leaving him swaying in terror and unable to turn round.

'Sometimes,' said a man next to me, 'there are sharks. It is the ships you see. The rubbish attracts them.' He settled to watch in anticipation of a gory cabaret and run through the fixed litany of questions I had come to expect. Where was I from? How long would I stay? English women, was it true they were cold though they slept with anyone? I fought back with my own list. What was his work? Where was he from?

'I,' he announced proudly, 'am Buginese. Look at my nose.' He turned his head sideways so that I would have the benefit of his profile. 'We Buginese have fine long noses like Europeans.' He rose. 'Ah, I believe I see a shark ... No it is just a shadow.' A pity.

There would be no floorshow.

'Will you eat a coconut?' Delighted. He whistled expertly and gestured with his fingers. There was a padding noise and a small boy appeared out of the darkness clutching coconuts by their tufts like trophy heads. He plonked them down together with two spoons and a cleaver and vanished again. My companion dealt the nuts a couple of blows of judicious violence, rather like a Japanese occupier not engaged in flower-arranging. The milk was fresh and slightly tart but rapidly cloying to a sticky mustiness. My long-nosed friend dug out slivers of meat with the cleaver, smooth and slippery like raw fish. 'Tomorrow,' he said, 'go out there to the island. It is a good place.' He nodded with his proud nose. When we had finished with the nuts, I returned the cleaver to the stall-holder. The nuts had already been paid for but it seemed proper to give him a hundred rupiahs for the use of the cleaver. His entire body became a machine for expressing joy. It is nice to be able to make someone's day for seven pence.

The motives of anthropologists, like those of others, do not stand close scrutiny. Field-work offers many satisfactions to the ethnographer. One is that he ceases to belong to the impoverished part of the population and becomes, in relative terms, a man of wealth – the sort of man who can blow seven pence in a gesture of sheer altruism. There is great pleasure in being able to bring a smile to other people's faces, a joy that is all the greater through being done with someone else's money, and very cheaply. All the Protestant virtues are simultaneously satisfied. Left-wing anthropologists are especially prone to the seductions of being able to behave like local gentry and dispense benefaction. It provides an immediate and entirely false feeling that you have got close to the people.

'Now,' said my friend, 'we will go to my house where there is a meeting to practise your language. You will give us a talk on

"First impressions of Indonesia". Try to keep it down to an hour.'

'An hour?'

'Yes. We have founded a group called the English Club. We meet for one hour most days. You will be able to meet my friends.'

I met his friends, and his cousins and his mother. I met a whole class of small boys in Muslim hats who were taken away from the Koran to talk to me in English. I answered questions about the royal family, traffic lights and the etiquette of eating asparagus, and gave a quick analysis of the shipbuilding industry. At the end of the evening, I fled back to the hotel.

'You will come again tomorrow?'

'I will see. I might leave for Toraja tomorrow.'

The next day was to be spent in making contacts and general preparation before 'plunging'. Unfortunately, it was a national holiday, the fortieth anniversary of the Indonesian declaration of independence. Almost everything was shut. The streets were filled with crocodiles of neat children being marched off to patriotic events. They raised little fists in the air, faces stern with nationalist fervour, and shouted, *Merdeka,* 'Freedom'. Then they collapsed in helpless giggles, reproved by a teacher who could not avoid smiling herself. Men wandered round town rather vaguely setting up flags, clutching aluminium poles like disoriented javelin-throwers. The highlight was a cycle-past, dominated by a bicycle transformed with silver foil into a torch of freedom. Unfortunately, there was a strong side-wind from the sea so that it wobbled all over the road and collided with a giant goldfish carried by eight little girls in an effort to promote fish as a source of protein. A man from the Ministry of Agriculture processed around town on a truck spraying water in the faces of the populace, while schoolboys dressed as stalks of rice danced to demonstrate their vigorous growth under the effects of insecticide. A sort of renegade exhibit existed in the form of a motorbike patiently converted into a giant snail. While its message was far from clear, it would suddenly appear from the most unexpected directions at high speed, swerve through the other floats and fall over. It was all terribly good-natured and showed that enviable Indonesian ability to find pleasure in the most unlikely places.

To get away from the heat and dust, I thought I might as well take a boat ride to an island a friend of mine had recommended. I was in terror of meeting the English Club. What had shaken me most was that the receptionist at the hotel had revealed herself to be a member. My movements would be closely watched. I caught a trishaw down to the harbour. The driver was given to garrulity.

'Toraja?' he said. 'I wouldn't go there. They eat human flesh you know.'

'How do you know?'

'*Everyone* knows.' That everyone hates the people 'next door' is about as close as you get to a universal in anthropology. This is strange in that the subject has always tended to assume that social interaction promotes solidarity *within* a people. The trishaw was equipped with electronic chimes that played 'We wish you a merry Christmas'. We sailed around the main square to 'bring us figgy pudding' and arrived at the quayside to 'and a happy new year'.

Tickets were on sale at the end of the pier, the prices doubled to mark the festive nature of the day. We set off in a small boat whose engine did not produce the expected noise but a series of quite discrete explosions like a senile incontinent. A child watched me with fascination and clutched my knees in sudden sticky affection. 'Tall!' it said. Mother and father laughed. From across the water came a dull boom as if the sound of the engine were echoing back. It had an oddly familiar ring that was hard to place. The boat swung broadside to accost a jetty and the sound suddenly gelled as the engine died. 'Oh baby. Erg fuddle tin fat swug. Oh yeah.' Oh Lord, it was the pop-group from the boat.

On the boat, they had been constrained and confined. Here they could spread themselves and let rip. A system of rasping loudspeakers conveyed their hymn of joy to the furthest reaches of the island. Not that those reaches reached very far. It was a small, crook-backed lump of sand dotted with temporary booths that sold sunglasses, gassy drinks and inflatable toys. A band of Chinese children were fishing for used condoms and lining them up on the beach beside the greasy water. A child emerged from the water covered in blood from a shark attack. But no, not a shark attack. A doting parent had daubed surface cuts with mercurochrome to produce this effect. A sign on the beach read, 'Beware much scrap iron'. After a swift turn round the island, the pop-group waving and playing louder in friendly greeting, I returned to the jetty waiting for the next boat back. A man with no shoes was fishing for prawns, patiently disentangling them from the rank growth of seaweed. We went through the usual questions.

'You should,' he said, 'meet my sister.'

In Africa, I would have known exactly what he meant but these were a proud people renowned for Muslim zeal. Possibly this man was a member of the English Club.

'Why?' I enquired nervously, expecting the stare people bestow upon the insane or foreign.

'She is a tea-towel lady.'

'Tea-towels. You mean she sells tea-towels? Batik?'

He laughed. 'No, no. She is a fanatic, very religious. She now wears a tea-towel on her head and refuses to go to the university. She will die with no husband. But you would find her interesting. She speaks good English.'

'Are you from Ujung Pandang?' Behind him a Buginese fishing boat putted past, its huge upcurving prow towering above the rest of the vessel. 'Wait,' I said, 'you are Buginese. I can tell by your fine, long nose.' Anthropology teaches you to make such links. They are called interpretation. He was delighted.

'Quite right!'

I found myself wondering whether Buginese refer to the prows of their ships as 'noses' or vice versa. There was an article somewhere on the symbolism of the Buginese vessel. I would have to look it up. But my friend had further data to offer.

'People here think a big nose means you have a big member. That's why women like them.' He blushed and covered his nose, a gesture of embarrassment I had seen elsewhere.

A boat of much perter snout arrived and we said goodbye. I embarked with a group of young fathers, bursting with pride in their progeny. Fathers and children hugged each other rapturously. To even look at their offspring made them almost explode with joy.

On the shore were two Australians, bleached and scorched from Bali, hairy-kneed and bare-footed. Although it was still early, they were very drunk as if in satire of cultural stereotypes, even waving bottles in fulfilment of their roles. The Indonesian fathers clutched their children tighter and hissed words of warning, needlessly for the tourists were discussing their bowels with the relish of tea-drinking mums talking of their plumbing.

'A bloody turd, mate,' roared one, 'the sort that just sits there and looks up at you. First I've dropped in bloody weeks.' They began to discuss whether copulation or defecation were the greater pleasure. They had obviously been long abroad and were habituated to the boldness that comes from being incomprehensible to the world at large. I ducked my head and tried to creep past shrouded in the fog of their scatological absorption. But it was not to be.

The boatman pointed at them, indicated me and shouted loudly, 'Look, friend!' It was probably the only English he knew but it was enough to make sure I was noticed. He nodded and grinned in the certainty of having done me a good turn. The Australians grinned too, lurching against the young fathers who hustled their children off, eyes smouldering. The tourists immediately recognized me as one of their kind, wishing to while away my time in beer-swilling mateship, examining in depth what it was that was *wrong* with the Indonesians and commenting pointedly on the people on the jetty. It took me nearly an hour to get away, leaving them shaking their heads over my Pommie bastard stuffed-shirt lack of warmth. Little boys squealed with delight as they threw their empty bottles into the harbour.

Tourists are the ugly face of every people. Is it the worst people who are tourists or does being a tourist bring out the worst? There is a nagging doubt that you are just the same as them, that – at least – you are perceived by locals as being the same. Tourism converts other people into stage properties that can be photographed and collected. I am not sure that at some level ethnography does not do the same. I have known anthropologists who regarded 'their' people as little more than laboratory animals, objects important to our own arrogant purposes, to be discarded or put back in their cages when they proved tedious or unduly bothersome. Yet, somehow, I felt there *had* been real human contact. People had been genuinely kind and helpful, put themselves out when there was no need, even made *me* behave a little better than I would have expected. A not unhappy thought with which to leave for the area where *real* ethnography was to be found. I somehow felt that Ujung Pandang was too hot for me.

The Ethnographic Frontier

'Touriis!' The child removed its finger from the nostril it had been industriously mining and pointed it at me. Then, taking advantage of the outstretched hand, it opened the palm and said, 'I ask for sweets. Give me money.' It was the first time I had heard what was an indissoluble union of ideas – tourist-sweets-money – cried at puttypersons by almost every child in Torajaland. Not that I had reached Torajaland proper as yet, I was on the coast in the town of Pare-Pare, poised to 'plunge'. The first Europeans took four hundred years to get from the coast to the mountains. The bus nowadays takes only hours but it still seems a long time.

My mendacious guidebook had vaunted the charms of the town but what had made me get off the bus was a building marked 'Museum'. It was the usual dowdy town, built alongside a dusty road where Chinese traders sold Japanese goods at inflated prices. A little way apart was the administrative area where civil servants maintained the integrity of the republic. To one side was a small port where rice was being loaded into Japanese ships. It is in small towns that one becomes aware of the enormously high proportion of Indonesians who are children. The investment in schools is tremendous. It is as if every third building is a school of some sort. There are three shifts in some schools every day, so that a treble tide of spotlessly uniformed children washes back and forth along main roads seemingly all the time. 'Hello Miss!' they shouted cheerfully.

I was billeted in a small inn built out over the water with little cubicles made of cardboard for rooms. As well as permitting everyone to hear what was happening in everyone else's room, their flimsy construction meant that it was possible to follow the vociferously prosecuted card game that raged nightly in the front hall. A complaint would have been unreasonable since an invitation to join in was always extended in the friendliest manner possible.

The best entertainment in town seemed to be next door in the tennis club where bureaucrats played with fierce determination to an incredibly high standard, attended by a host of urchins and judges, all of whom uttered loud cries of vicarious triumph or outrage. From dawn to dusk, they warred across the net, nostrils flared, snarling and guffawing.

The only other distraction was the arrival of a large German tourist who intimidated the management with his spade-like beard. Whenever he sat on a chair or bed, it would crumple beneath him. Curiously, the owner regarded this as very funny.

'See,' he would say, holding up two sections of a chair, 'he has done it again.'

Another curiosity was the bathroom. As is usually the case in South East Asia, the source of water was a cement tank from which water was to be enthusiastically splashed over the body. The receptacle was shared with the bathroom next door, the wall coming down like a curtain into the water. It was also the home, however, of a large black goldfish of phlegmatic demeanour. When it saw that someone was in occupancy on one side, it would swim, averting its gaze, to the other side. If both sides were occupied, it was forced into a fearful oscillation. The owner was amazed that the hirsute German doggedly refused to use the bathroom except when both sides were empty out of consideration for the fish. He seemed to think that Europeans had a religious detestation of fish as Muslims do of pigs.

Visiting the museum was more difficult than had been foreseen. I embarked in a trishaw and set off with a driver of great antiquity. There is always a certain delicacy and ambivalence in such a situation. People stare. But are they thinking 'See! There is that lazy puttyman riding on the back of that poor elder, who is old enough to be his father'? Or are they saying, 'See! It is good that he has hired that old man instead of a younger one who would be faster'?

The trishaw driver himself spoke as one about to go out of business. The government was about to abolish trishaws in town and replace them with taxis. But why? Who knew why the government did things. He would have to go and live at the charge of his son who had little enough land as it was. He had saved for years to own his own trishaw instead of sharing the takings with an owner. Now, how could he sell it? He would have to take it apart and sell the wheels, one by one. It was a devastatingly depressing picture – the old man selling first the wheels, then the saddle, then the bell, with ever-decreasing profit.

He pedalled slowly south on the tarmac road, the whole frame of the machine heaving from side to side with the effort applied by the legs. Motorized traffic burred past us honking indignantly. Fellow-pedallers rang their bells to express the community of their endeavour. To either side of the road, the concrete blocks of commerce gave way to fine, wooden houses on stilts, shaded by palms, simple and spacious with a hard, bare, somehow masculine quality as if disdaining flounces. People stood in chest-high concrete or wickerwork enclosures and poured water over themselves or leaned over balconies, contemplating the world through a haze of cigarette smoke.

The museum was locked and deserted save for an idiot boy. It seems an immutable rule of nature that museums are always manned by an idiot youth in the way that departmental secretaries in universities are always madwomen. The trishaw driver was outraged on my behalf, demanded to know the whereabouts of the custodian, negotiated a new contract to take me there and set off railing against the world in general.

We went to a building loud with the flags of the Republic, were introduced to an extremely polite group of gentlemen and required to fill in the inevitable visitors' book. Only then was it made clear that the man with the key had returned to the museum and could now be found there. After elaborate, friendly farewells, we returned to the trishaw. As I re-embarked, I suddenly became chillingly aware of a wind around the buttocks. I had ripped my trousers from stem to stern on the trishaw canopy and lay open to the world.

Going round a museum with one's behind always pointing to the wall, is an exercise fit to be set to a future Prince of Wales. It is excessively difficult.

The museum was dedicated to the royal house of the town and revealed it to have been wealthy enough to import the worst trade goods from East and West. Cheap Chinese plates jostled Dutch vases and extraordinarily bad carvings from across the sea in Borneo. The collection was lived in and among by the curator and his wife. He was a very gentle and soft-spoken man. She bore a striking resemblance to Bette Davis in her later roles as a beslippered, whisky-voiced slattern.

The curator's taste ran to tales of wonder. He spoke of a cannon that fired, unprimed, to announce the death of a member of the house. He had sought to transport it to the museum but it always returned unaided to the top of the hill. He had heard stones scream and seen ghosts in ancient dress. The ordinary-looking knives in that cupboard over there were magic. Once drawn, they could not be sheathed until they had tasted blood. Bette nodded silent agreement or intervened to mend the tale.

A donation was solicited and given. Bette smoked endless cigarettes with gestures of world-weary cynicism and scuffed around in tatty slippers. As befits one leaving royalty in torn trousers, I bowed out backwards.

Across the road stood a sign, 'To the beach'. A stony path ran off between the palm-trees, threading between wooden stilt houses, balconies bright with sarongs hung out to dry.

Here at last was the beach of my familiar tropic isle fantasies. It was suitably fringed with coconuts, wooden fishing boats riding at anchor. The sea was calm and blue, unruffled by waves and merely toyed with the sand. A child appeared. It yawned, 'Give me money.' I delivered a little homily on the nature of shame that it listened to stonily. There was a man crouched at the sea edge doubtless engaged in some act of old sea doggery. I approached, greeting on my lips. Becoming suddenly aware of an alien presence, he swung round with a look of horror, literally girt up his loins and made off at speed, splashing through the tepid water. It was all too clear what he had been at. I now knew what the toilet arrangements were here.

I fled in the opposite direction and became aware of another man playing peek-a-boo between the trees. I would not make the same mistake twice and sternly looked the other way. It was his turn to creep up on me.

'Good day,' he bellowed.

'Good day.'

'Two hundred rupiahs please.'

'What for?'

'Tourist tax.' He whipped out a peaked cap from behind his back and held out a receipt, grinning bashfully like a swain offering flowers.

'Do not bathe over there. There are sea urchins.' I did not understand the word so he engaged in an elaborate mime of a man stung on one foot.

'The water here is good?'

'Very good. It is warm because of that.' He indicated a stone breakwater.

Children were swimming around like turtles in big, black inner tubes, shouting ethnic insults at each other.

'Chinese got no nose.'

'Buginese face like a goat.'

No remarks were made about puttypersons. I paddled experimentally, trouser legs rolled up. I should be wearing a knotted handkerchief on my head but they would not know about that. The water was deliciously warm like a restorative footbath. Turning back towards the shore. I saw why. The breakwater housed a large iron pipe. It was the town sewer and I was paddling in warm effluent.

But even in so apparently unprofitable a place, there were signs that Indonesia would prove a fertile field for ethnographic enquiry. I went to a small shop that advertised crab soup.

'No crab soup. No crab,' said the waiter.

'Why no crab?' The beach was aswarm with fishermen, boats, shells of molluscs.

'I don't know. We always say because of the full moon. I don't know why. If you want to ask the fisherman he's in the kitchen.'

Sure enough, there he sat drinking coffee, a tiny wizened man, burned deep brown by the sun, his skin hanging in loose folds at all the joints as though it had been borrowed from someone considerably larger. I asked about crabs and the full moon.

'Quite right,' he said. 'There are no crabs at the full moon. They are all menstruating.'

'Rubbish,' said a cook, laughing. 'Crabs are all male, they don't menstruate.'

'It's the light,' said one of the waiters. 'Crabs don't like the light. They go and hide in the deep water so you can't catch them.'

'Not so,' said another cook, sitting down. 'It's like this. The moon pulls on the sea and makes waves. Crabs don't like the rough water so they go and hide under rocks.' The entire restaurant had by now come to a halt. It was a refreshing change from my last people in Africa who were deeply conservative and resisted speculation about the justification of ancestral wisdom.

The fisherman shook his head in perplexity. 'Wah!' he said. 'What it is to be educated, to have read books. You see, I'm just a simple fisherman. We don't know anything about all this. We can't even go fishing when it's the full moon because all our wives are menstruating.' It seemed the point at which I had come in.

Back at the hotel, I was suddenly impatient of delays and determined to leave at once for the mountains where the Toraja were to be found. The term apparently means little more than 'hillman' and is from the Buginese. Doubtless, therefore, it is an ethnic slur-word and the present confusion about who is and who is not a Torajan probably derives from the fact that they traditionally had no such name for themselves. I would start with the town of Mamasa. I went to the bus station.

'Mamasa?'

'Polmas.'

'Er ... yes, but Mamasa?'

'Polmas ... You get in bus.' I sought Polmas in vain on my map.

'Where is Polmas?' The querulous voice asking the obvious. No answer.

'Is Polmas near Mamasa?'

He shrugged. 'Yes, near.'

'How near? Can I get from Polmas to Mamasa in one day?'

'Oh yes. You get in bus.'

'Certain?'

'Yes. You get in bus now.' I did not believe a word of it but what are you to do? They were friendly people. I had coin of the realm and would not starve. Ignoring the proffered front seat (more expensive, more likely to be sick), I clambered in the open back. We set off.

We set off up to a point. Rather, we roamed the town looking for people who looked as though they might want to go to Polmas – wherever that might be. We cruised languorously up and down the main road, seeking to entice those who might be yet in doubt. We honked the horn at *cewek* and leaned out grinning. We accosted anyone carrying a heavy load, displaying with spread arms the space available.

'See! There is yet room. Mount! Come with us to Polmas.'

I say *we* for no distinction was made between crew and passengers. It was accepted that we were now engaged in some common enterprise, that our fortunes were inextricably mixed. Passengers leapt deftly down to assist new arrivals with their baggage. We made room. We shared cigarettes. Suddenly, we were a band of brothers. Bags of rice were embarked, children materialized in droves and were packed among the chattels like china. We set off towards the mountains in high good spirits – and returned to the bus station to collect more passengers. We drove around looking for someone's brother, picked him up and returned to his house for more luggage. Finally, when it seemed that all hope of departure today was lost, we set our backs to the coast and rattled off towards the darkening mountains.

Somewhere along that road, there lies an invisible frontier. It is first apparent in the surface. The tarmac peters out. It becomes dirt. The dirt gives way to bare rock over which the bus bucks and heaves. At points are huge yellow machines, radiators snarling with Japanese characters, busy pulverizing stone and spewing it across the road. But soon they give way to an untamed wilderness where the road is not a channel to communication but a barrier to it. Two things spread the ketchup of Western culture across the planet. One is communication. The other is its most powerful metaphor – money. But here, we were quite suddenly in another world, one that looked inward not outward, where material comforts could not be taken for granted but where there was the exciting possibility of glimpsing an alien vision of reality. To anyone hooked on the ethnographic quest, that is the greatest possible excitement. I asked a question of the man next to me, the litmus paper of our state.

'What time will we arrive?'

He shrugged. 'How can I know?'

I was right. We had crossed the frontier. He tunnelled down into his corner seat, wrapped his arms around me without further acquaintance and settled to sleep, breathing contentedly against my neck. This was another world. I draped myself around him and soon fell asleep too.

'Touriis!' It was dark. An awareness of bitter cold. Touriis!' A woman calling. The engine had stopped and the passengers were all crawling out of the van looking intensely crapulous. I thought it worth the investment of time to scowl at the woman. She smiled back, patting a small boy who had run up and was also grinning.

'Her son,' explained a yawning fellow passenger, 'is called Turis. She had him when a stranger was passing through the village and she liked the word.'

Turis looked at me but did not ask for money or sweets. It was a medieval scene, a caravan of pack-horses had come to meet the bus and boxes were being unloaded under flaring torches by men with cloaks wrapped around their shoulders. They pulled out swords to hack at the fastenings.

'Come and drink coffee,' said the woman. 'I must light the lamps. The electricity goes off at ten.'

We stretched and yawned, mimed comic shivers and shuffled across to a bare concrete house that stood stark on the top of the mountain, limpid starlight washing down on it. The driver was already inside pumping an oil-lamp. Some stopped to urinate against the wall. As we passed through the door, the electricity went out and the corners of the room shrank down around us to a cosy dusk. In the kitchen a sort of shadow play produced hot coffee.

'Please no sugar.'

'No sugar?' The entire kitchen gathered to watch this wonder.

'You drink coffee with no sugar?' The Indonesians were ladling five or six spoonfuls into each cup. They watched as I drank as if suspecting some last-minute substitution.

'Truly Dutchmen are strange.'

'I am not Dutch. I am English.'

'Are not all puttymen the same? We call them all Dutch.'

'Are the Buginese and the Torajans the same?' They understood that all right. I suddenly realized that it was pitch dark and I still did not know where I was going. The driver had a map.

'What is the name of this place?'

'It has no name. It is just a house.'

'Where is it?'

'Polmas.'

'Where do you go next?'

'Further, Polmas.'

'But ...' Then the penny dropped. They had taken the names at the two ends of the road, Polewali and Mamasa, combined them and used them for the whole region. I was *in* Polmas and going to Polmas.

We sat in Polmas and ate little cakes brought by the mother of Turis. Again, the usual questions. My little-learned Indonesian was brought out and paraded like a spoilt child before visitors. Several of the passengers were schoolteachers. In the Third World, they are always travelling. They could translate between Indonesian and Torajan, a quite distinct language, and also knew some Dutch which did us no good. I thought of some children I had once known in Cameroon who had learned Norwegian in the hope that it would open up to them a new world of communication.

At least I did not have to explain my trade. There were, it seemed, other anthropologists about.

'Up in the north, there is the French lady. She was once very beautiful but I think she is now old. In the west is the American. He speaks our language very well. Then there is the American girl but I think she only speaks English though she is close to God. Then there are the Dutch. They have children.'

'Their own children?'

'No. Torajan children. Our children are very beautiful. That is why we adopt each other's children. I was adopted when I was small. Perhaps you will stay here and marry a Torajan girl and adopt children. I have seven, you can have some of mine.'

'I will take all seven. You can make some more.' We all laughed. I looked at Turis's ears. They were not in the least pointed. I had been misled.

We set off again, rumbling and rolling. The driver had used the stop to repair the cassette-player. It wailed the same six songs over and over again. Outside, giant ferns waved their fronds at us.

It was long past midnight when we reached Mamasa and pulled up outside the only hotel, a wooden shack whose doors were firmly locked. I stood helplessly outside. They took pity on me.

'Is there anybody there?' cried the driver, knocking on the moon-lit door. A chain reaction of barking spread over the mountains. He knocked again. A tiny, wobbly light appeared in one corner of the house and trembled closer. The driver shook me firmly by the hand.

'There is someone coming. You will be all right. Sleep well.'

He revved hard and shot off with a screech. I was the only one left who could be held responsible for all this disruption. A large number of bolts were adjusted and a sleepy face peered at me.

'I'm very sorry ...' I began.

'Tomorrow,' he said. Talking was too much effort. I caught a vision of rows of bottles and stools made of tree-trunks and was led up a vertical ladder to a small room of pine. He waited till I had lit the candle and then walked silently away. The dogs were still disputing which should have the last bark.

HORSE-TRADING

The guidebook describes Mamasa as 'Tyrolean'. It is surrounded by mountains but not the sporty alpine sort of Austria. They are glowering woody slopes with rashes of bare red earth. Still, the adjective is justified by the presence of two white, steepled, wooden churches at the entrance to the valley in which houses are lined up along a purling brook. It is clean, rural, cool.

But there was something not mentioned in the guidebook. In this remote mountain valley, there was a conference of church youth choirs.

Christianity is a religion with many faces. It may be frowzily ceremonial, embarrassingly emotional, frostily ascetic. Each culture takes what it likes from the religion it is offered. In the export of date-expired religions from the West, one factor has constantly impressed the Torajans about Christianity – the possibility of forming choirs. Their traditional religion makes much use of choral singing in an extensive repertoire of songs for all occasions. The arrival of church singing and the guitar have allowed this ancient root to blossom. In the evening, Torajan towns resound to the strum of instruments and the lilt of voices. On Sundays, they shake to the power of flexed vocal cords.

Morning is always the time when one's cultural relativity is sorely tried. We are all xenophobic at that hour. It is a time of firm prejudice and heightened sensitivities. The sight of others sucking in large quantities of garlic and rice for breakfast is always hard to take. The cheerful generosity with which they offer to share it with a foreign traveller would at all other times be endearing. In the morning, it leaves you feeling grumpily disagreeable. The inn was crowded with young people, beautiful, smiling, friendly as puppies. They offered me garlic. In my urgent need for coffee, they sang me a hymn – just for me – at deafening volume and with grinning gusto. The young ladies showed me how exquisitely their voices could trill. The young men flaunted their bass resonance and perfect teeth. I felt old, seamy, hung over from travel – above all, betrayed. For I had not come so far to meet Christians, to see people who doggedly refused to accept the picturesqueness I wanted to thrust upon them. Where were their strange customs and odd rites? The only odd thing about these people was how they could be so totally nice and unremarkable.

Over the other side, sat two men of a different kind, hunched over the coffee as if the music scalded their ears as it did mine. We grimaced at each other in mute sympathy. One extended a hand hospitably towards a tree-trunk stool. I joined them.

'You like the music?' one asked.

'It's a little loud.'

'They are Christian. You are Christian too I think.'

'A sort of Christian.' In Indonesia, only the criminally insane have no religious affiliation. What were these men? Possibly, the old pagan religion. I brightened.

'We,' said the other, 'are Muslims.'

'Torajans?' They held up their hands in horror.

'No. We are Buginese from the coast. We are schoolmasters.' The term was being lobbed into the conversation like a hand grenade. It was calculated to evoke respect, not the reaction of a Godfrey Butterfield MA.

Another choir, summoned by the sound of their confreres,

appeared in the door. It was a mark of their spirit of Christian fellowship that they immediately abandoned their own hymn to join in that of the first group. By now, we were conversing in hoarse bellows.

'Is it not difficult to live in a Christian town?' I inquired.

'No. We are all one nation now.' Pancasila – the five principles of the national ideology – just what one would expect from a schoolmaster.

'Only occasionally is there trouble.' He leaned forward and his voice subsided to a confidential yell.

'The last time was when the mobile cinema showed that anti-Christian film.'

'Which film?'

He groped as if pulling spiders' webs out of his hair. 'The one that showed Christ as a dirty, drug-crazed hippy.' *Hippy.* They knew the word.

'What was it called?' He consulted with his friend.

'Jesus Christ Film-star.'

'Superstar?'

'Yes. That's it. There was fighting. They said it must be made by Muslims.'

'I don't think that can be right.'

'The other time was when I told the children that the bodies of Muslim saints do not rot.'

'But we say the same about Christian saints.'

'I know, but that is because God wishes to preserve the example of their wickedness for the instruction of the faithful.'

I fled the world religions and sauntered around a sort of village green with a football pitch at which goats chewed. The road led on through rice-fields, snaking along the bottom of the valley with long grass growing up through the sandy soil like a nineteenth-century watercolour of the English countryside. Horses stood glumly in the fields – up to their fetlocks in water – as though being punished. It was a beautiful day of gentle heat cooled by a soft wind. Everywhere was cascading water. Up on the hills were little bamboo windmills clicking and whirring. A horseman approached on a diminutive steed that danced and bucked under him. We laughed at each other and I offered a cigarette. He adjusted his sword and dug out an ancient flint lighter.

'Where have you come from?'

He gestured into the hills with a thumb.

'I have come to the market to sell my wife's cloth.' He indicated the cloak of faded orange he was wearing.

'They still weave cloth up there?'

'Oh yes. You will see at the market tomorrow, if you go there.'

I indicated the windmills. 'What are they for?'

He looked peevishly up at the hills. 'Oh, just a toy. For the children.'

We parted and I walked over a roofed wooden bridge with seats sunk into the sides like church pews. Two little girls came up and held my hands in rather shocking trust, one each side like in the pictures of Jesus suffering little children. Almond eyes of limpid innocence stared into mine.

'Give me some sweets. I want money.'

'Sweets will rot your teeth.'

An old lady working in a garden cackled approvingly. 'Quite right. They should be ashamed.' They did not look ashamed but ran off giggling and blowing raspberries.

'Good day, mother.'

'Good day. Where are you staying?' I explained and we went through the usual questions. 'Where does this road lead, mother?'

'Into the mountains. To Bittuang if you want. There is a fine house about two kilometres along. You should go there.'

On impulse I pointed at the windmills and asked, 'What are

those for?'

She smirked, showing mahogany-coloured teeth. 'Those make the wind for cleaning the rice.'

I passed on, feeling increasingly like a traveller in a fairy-tale.

The road abandoned all pretence of being an English country lane and assumed a cobbled surface oddly at variance with the banana groves on either side. Above the trees appeared the roof of a house, a ponderous curved structure of wooden tiles.

Torajan houses are justly famous. They are huge constructions of wood, raised off the ground on stilts, cunningly jointed and pegged, their whole surface magnificently carved and painted in intricate designs, buffalo heads, birds, leaves. They may be hundreds of years old and are the fixed points by which people work out their personal relationships. They face north, the direction associated with the ancestors, and before many is a pillar running up to the roof ridge on which are stacked the horns of buffalo killed at festivals. Directly facing the house are its rice-barns, smaller versions of the same structure. Under the main storage area is a platform on which people sit and engage in the small but vital acts of social life. Here, all can gossip and receive friends, women weave their cloths, men repair their tools, guests sleep.

A group of men sat cross-legged and watched me approach., We exchanged greetings and they invited me to sit. Again, I cursed my lace-up shoes that had to be laboriously unknotted when removed to enter anyone's private space. Having exchanged cigarettes and established my identity as a Christian Englishman, we moved on to the staggering fact that rice did not grow in my country, therefore we had no rice-barns to sit on. Would I like to visit the house? An alarmed face spotted our approach from a small hatch some twenty feet off the ground and disappeared in a scamper of feet. I laboured awkwardly up the ladder and past a door carved with a deep image of a buffalo head.

The house was divided into a number of small rooms with raised sills like the watertight compartments of a boat. Along two sides ran an open gallery – again like the deck of a boat. No wonder that early travellers had suggested to the Torajans that their houses were modelled on the ships of some original migration – a view of things they have now come to believe; after all, anthropologists should know best. The shutters were open to admit a little light that streamed with motes of dust like the light in a church. The ancient walls were decorated with pictures of Western film stars torn from magazines and hand-tinted photographs of marriage scenes, the faces rendered bulbous and unrecognizable as if painted from a description only. We went on a tour. In one room, a cat dozed contentedly in the ashes of a fire. In another, a stick-like arm hung through the mosquito-net shrouding a bed.

'My father,' explained the man. 'He wants to greet you but he is ill.'

I shook the hand with its rasping, paper-thin skin, hot and dry. Eyes glowed redly in the darkness. Thin white lips muttered politenesses. We returned to the entry room and sat on blue-painted cane chairs. Such houses were not made for furniture and its intrusion makes them cramped and ungainly. Coffee was brought – incredibly sweet – its cloyingness not mitigated by the cakes of red palm-sugar served throughout Torajaland as a token of hospitality. It felt good to have got away from the tourist round and met these good, simple people. The subject of my marriage state came round again. The sheer inevitability of marriage in Indonesia makes the unwedded or even divorced state incomprehensible. If children seem unwilling to sort out such things for themselves, the parents move in. I have known Indonesians in Europe terrified to go home even for a short visit on the grounds that they would be kidnapped and find themselves wed overnight. One of the most useful accessories of the anthropological trade is a picture to be carried in one's wallet. It depicts a blonde, heavy-breasted woman whose dress is simultaneously decorous yet suggestive of vast charms. It is invaluable evidence for getting you out of all sorts of difficulties or for initiating discussions of marriage practices. It can be explained as representing one's wife or sister, even – given the notable inability of those from other cultures to accurately guess the age of Westerners – one's daughter. The only problem with such deception is that you rapidly lose track of those settings in which you are wed and those in which you are unwed. Informants too have an unfortunate habit of talking to each other. For this reason alone, such ploys are best used in casual encounters only but can be a valuable short-cut when you simply cannot face going through the whole business of marriage in Europe yet again. Nevertheless, this was a welcome opportunity for some gentle ethnography.

In my country, I declared, we did not pay for our wives. Yes, it was the same in other parts of Toraja – though not here where women were respected – which was why the Buginese liked to marry Torajan women from other areas. In my country we paid money on divorce. Same here. In my country, however, if a poor man married a rich woman, he might ask money from her. They looked pitying. How could we allow people from one class to marry another? Of course it would not work. Anyway, a woman should never marry beneath her for the sake of her children, since her status determined that of hear offspring. We were well into an analysis of the class and marriage system – a difficult job like teasing the bones out of a fish – when my informant became increasingly confused and inconsistent. The moment to stop. But he did not want to.

'Wait,' he said, 'I'll check.' He slipped into the next room to ask his father, I assumed, and I felt a pang of guilt that the poor old man should be disturbed. Soon, he re-emerged thumbing into a large blue-bound book.

'Here you are. It's all in here.'

It was his thesis on the marriage system, examined and approved at the university in Ujung Pandang. He was an anthropologist.

As I left, he produced a visitor's book in which I was invited to write my name, my reaction to the house and – gentle hint – the size of my contribution to its upkeep. I noted with disapproval that a party of thirty American anthropology students had been round the month before. Torajaland began to feel very crowded. There was an urge to get my own back for my disappointed expectations. I indicated the windmills up on the hills.

'What are those for?' I asked casually. He frowned.

'Odd you should ask that. I've noticed that however many times you ask the old people about them, you seem to get a different answer every time. It's my belief that they are simply a marker of time at the harvest, part of a wider complex involving stick-fighting and the use of spinning tops but it's not impossible that they have a material function in scaring away birds.' Totally defeated, I retired.

Back at the inn, the young Christians had evaporated like the morning dew. Only the disorder of the furniture and a slightly acrid whiff of vomit betokened the excesses of youthful piety. The family of the proprietor and I were the only occupants, together with a deaf mute who wandered in and a Japanese construction-worker who spoke no Indonesian. The Japanese showed tearful pictures of the family he had forsaken to come and work on the road. I was tempted to get out my blonde woman but refrained. The son of the house discussed the dangers of flying in eloquent gesture with the deaf mute, while I did the son's English homework. The next day, it came back heavily corrected. It was full of incomprehensible questions such as, 'Is the moon at seven o'clock or behind the door?'

Meanwhile, the wayward daughter of the house spent the evening pulling white hairs out of the head of the Japanese. Her excess of makeup, the clearly half-European child she had returned with from Bali despite the absence of a husband, allotted her fairly firmly to the local category of 'wicked woman'. She regarded me purposefully throughout the evening while I refused to notice her attention.

Abruptly, she spoke, 'I have a friend who knows you well.'

I feigned polite interest. 'In Indonesia?'

'Yes. In Indonesia too. They know you very well.' The pronoun did not reveal the sex of the person in question.

'Is your friend male or female?'

She smiled knowingly. 'A little of both.' She cradled the head of the construction-worker in her hands.

A transvestite? Not the actress from the theatre in Jakarta?

She continued, 'But my friend wants to know you better and has given me a message for you.' She tweaked another white hair from the crown of the Japanese.

I tired of this mysterious mode of communication carried on literally over the head of the Japanese. 'Look,' I said, 'who is your friend and just what is the message?' She giggled, let go of the head so that the poor man nearly fell on the floor and danced across the room to slap down a piece of paper before me.

'This is the message,' she beamed. 'My friend is Jesus.' It was a religious tract.

Since it was market-day, the goats had been reluctantly persuaded to yield tenancy of the football pitch to heaps of produce from the surrounding countryside. Strange, lumpy vegetables like cancerous growths and sliced jackfruit like sections of brain were heaped up in pallid, glistening mounds. The wooden shops had thrown open their folding doors and displayed the cheap goods of China and Japan, canned mackerel, scented soap, matches, keyrings showing girls whose bras dropped off when they were held upside down. From the very middle of the throng, a staccato voice fed through a whistling loudspeaker seduced the credulous through an obstacle course. If you ducked under ropes and over cables, leapt heaps of tomatoes and slithered through pools of effluent you came to the still centre.

There you would find a huckster-healer, peddling powders that cured everything from dysentery to infertility. At one point, all the ladies were sent away so that the delicate problem of 'male weakness' could be raised. The focus of attention was a sensational plastic torso whose organs could be scooped out to demonstrate the malady in question. In concession to popular taste, it was in the form of a blonde Western woman with enormous clip-on breasts, and hair that could be pulled out in clumps as an aid in the discussion of dandruff.

Apart from this, the material culture on display was more than a little disappointing. A few dispiriting cloths were on offer, the dyes now strictly chemical. The most expensive was of rayon. As I peered disconsolately through the pile, I felt someone slip a hand under my shirt and begin tickling me. Spinning round, I looked into the grinning face of the horseman from yesterday. In a gesture worthy of Errol Flynn, he spun his tubular cloak around his neck so that it hung down his back and hugged me to his bosom.

'If you want cloths,' he whispered, 'come with me.'

Soon we were in a wooden coffee shop in a thick fug of clove-scented cigarette smoke. The patrons were mountain people, short, wiry, thick-haired and wizened. The men wore their cloaks up around their ears like bats and cloths were pulled out from under the table, bundles of them tied up with string. They were bright red and orange with stripes of cardwork patterning. The colours were natural and would fade gently.

'From the plants,' said my guide, touching the colours with the tips of his fingers. We began to bargain. It was a gentle business. Once more, it struck me how unlike African bargaining it was – the absence of aggression and furious posing. We pushed prices back and forth in a curiously disinterested way, a bit like wine-tasters swilling vintages over their palates. Soon we had agreed and I had a fine new cloak. But the encounter had given birth to another idea. I would hire a horse and head up into the mountains.

There is a tradition in anthropology that the amount of physical suffering of the researcher is a measure of the value of his data. Like many other presuppositions, it is tenacious in the face of good negative evidence. Another such idea is that, beneath the complex surface where traditional and modern meet, there lies a layer of *real* ethnography, the pure uncorrupted Indonesia. If you can only get far enough from towns, you will surely find it. From this perspective, a horse-ride into the forest seemed like a good idea.

I have never liked horses. My experience of riding them is small and dismal. They intuitively know that you are frightened of them.

I spent a great deal of time over the next couple of days talking to people in town. Just as the difficulty of haggling is enormously increased if you have absolutely no idea of what is a reasonable price, so it is extremely awkward to pick out the best horses for a journey when you have little idea of what a good horse looks like or even what your destination is.

People told me of villages in the hills where there were ancient houses, where people were still pagans, where blacksmiths had strange habits. It seemed all I had to do was head north. I spent even more time looking at horses. I guessed that excessively thin mounts and those with large festering sores on their backs were best avoided. Intuition suggested I should look at their hooves, so I did that without quite knowing what I was looking for. The owners, however, definitely expected it. The proverb told me I should at all costs look at their teeth so I did that too. It was much like the ways, in the past. I had pretended competence before the owners of second-hand cars I might buy. What they did not know, however, was that I had long abandoned all hope of judging horseflesh. It was the owners I was judging.

There is obviously some deep kinship between horse traders and second-hand car dealers. Both categories seem to hold an undue number of deeply shifty characters with large bundles of currency hidden about their persons. Prices never seemed to be simple. It was always a matter of a certain sum paid now with a discount for this and that and a need for careful calculation. Arithmetic seemed to enter some strange new domain. I found it hard to understand why one person should require a minimum of three horses. Only at the last minute did I discover that one trader was proposing to charge me extra for the use of a saddle. When I asked who was responsible for horse-feed they stared at me blankly.

'Horses eat grass,' one explained gently. What about food for myself, for a guide, blankets, cigarettes? They shrugged. That was up to me. As for themselves, they would take nothing and expect nothing. They would rely on me.

Finally, I found the right man for the job, one with the splendid name of Darius. There was no mistaking his open, frank face, the straight look in his eyes, the lively intelligence – the good Indonesian. We squatted down beside the horses' hooves I had just finished looking at and shared a cigarette. I explained the nature of my expedition. He nodded in understanding. There were interesting people in the hills, and fine houses too. I would be all right with him. He understood that I was new to this country and would need help. The horses were good. I would ride this one – see how fat it was. We could leave tomorrow. Meet at the bridge at 5.30 a.m.

THIS TOWN
AIN'T BIG ENOUGH
FOR BOTH OF US

It did not come as a great surprise to be still sitting under the bridge at 6.30. *Rubber time* is a fact of life even the Indonesians make jokes about. The system whereby 5.30 is expressed as 'half-six' is often misunderstood and meetings are fraught with difficulty. I was *under* the bridge for the reason that it was pouring with rain, big wet blobs spattering down that had shown the roof of the bridge to be full of holes. There was a distant jingling of harness and I looked up hopefully. But it was not Darius. I looked down into the brown water gushing underneath as the horses slipped and juddered on the planks behind me and came to a halt, tossing their heads and steaming.

I turned to see a slightly benevolent garden gnome, swathed in a plastic waterproof of Lincoln Green. Time stretched out between us. He coughed. I tried a greeting and discovered, as I had expected, that he spoke hardly any Indonesian and furthermore had no teeth. I looked at the horses again, while the gnome looked doubtful. Perhaps he wanted me to look at their hooves. The lead horse looked much as Torajan horses normally do, short, shaggy, resentful. It eyed me appraisingly and its lips curled. The second was almost invisible beneath a pile of plastic jerrycans. The third was familiar. Surely this was the chubby beast selected as my mount?

'Where is Darius?'

The gnome rustled, finally extricated an arm and pointed up into the hills. He pointed at himself and me and indicated the same direction.

'He has gone on ahead?' The gnome gurgled assent. It was the moment I had dreaded. I had to get on.

Circling the beast suggested no obvious way of ingress. Wait a minute, there was something wrong here. There were no stirrups. Moving round to the front to adjust the reins. I found there were none of those either.

'How do I get on?' A burr of indistinct vowels was followed by the Indonesian for 'jump'. I jumped and ended up prone across its back. Horses automatically know when they have an idiot aboard. Mine chose this moment to move off and cannon into the horse in front, which turned round and bit it. The saddle was unlike any I had ever encountered before. It seemed to consist of a bundle of firewood, cut wide to splay the legs out and covered with sacking. It was loose, twisting round under me and depositing me back on the ground. Fortunately, Torajan horses are less than half as big as Western horses so it was no great distance to tumble. It was unfortunate that the beast in front was backing up. It promptly bore down on me and stamped away about my head like a Scottish dancer. Ignoring the chance to inspect its hooves. I rolled whimpering out of the way while the gnome wrestled with the pile of jerrycans and cursed.

It was clearly the moment to take charge and set the course in which our relationship would run. At such times, language difficulties count for nothing. I stood up and explained that I had never ridden a horse before and would require instruction. The gnome grunted. A small appreciative crowd had now gathered, of the sort that any minor incident can summon. Fortunately, Torajan children are not shy and one emerged to explain the basic controls. A child of about ten, he swung himself into the saddle with insolent grace and explained that you had to grip with your knees. The hands should grasp the front of the firewood saddle. In moments of stress such as swimming rivers (was I going to be swimming rivers?) it was best to simply dig your fingers into the mane. The horse knew the words for 'left' and 'right' in Indonesian.

'Thank you. Now tell me how I start it – no, how I stop it first.' He reached forward and grabbed a handful of hair on the horse's forelock and wrenched its head round shouting, 'Stop!' It seemed likely to work. The horse was totally submissive. He leapt lithely down. I attempted to replace him. It was like one of those pathetic spectacles at holiday camps where aged grannies are persuaded to ape the movements of dancing girls. The child sighed and went to the roadside where he pulled out a dagger and cut an enormous stick.

'To start, you beat the horse with this and shout "whoosh".' I tried a few delicate 'whooshes' without the stick.

'No, not like that. *Whoosh*,' he screamed and gave the horse a mighty slap on the rump. With a neck-jolting jerk, we lurched off, me scrabbling for a foothold, a kneehold – anything. The crowd hooted in joyful derision. The motion was exceedingly unpleasant. Opposite corners of the beast seemed to rise simultaneously so there was no place of rest on the firewood raft. The gnome and the jerrycan horse galloped up behind and overtook. It seemed we had already set off. Under the green plastic hood was a gigantic smirk.

We rode for twelve hours that day without stopping. The road stretched ahead, depressingly visible for miles, a vivid red scar across the landscape. At first we followed the gentle contours of the valley through a light and not unrefreshing rain. Soon, we struck uphill. Fields dwindled and disappeared. After half an hour of steady climbing, we were in the forest. It was not the rain-forest I had known in Africa, a cool and shady place. Here it was dank and steamy. Every plant seemed to have sharp or spiky leaves, to reach forward to slice at your flesh. It was surprising to see the house-plants that had to be cajoled into reluctant growth in England. Here, they were disgustingly fecund with thick green leaves. You felt that if you stopped they would swarm all over you.

On a more used trail there would have been bridges. Instead, every few miles would come the roar of water followed by a slow descent, the horses jumping and skidding down wet rocks to the river itself. At this time of year the torrents were low, so the horses just plunged in up to their haunches and felt their way across the stony bottom. Always at the low point would be a thick cloud of mosquitoes or butterflies that settled and drank your sweat.

The horse submitted me to subtle tests. It rapidly learned that when cries of 'whoosh' failed to accelerate it. I would be strangely reluctant to use the sapling. It slowed down to a dawdle. Hoping to make a truce between us, I inquired its name. The gnome mumbled something like 'Bugger me'. The horse responded to it and broke into a trot. Little bits of technique began to emerge. I found that it was easier to lean backwards when going down the slopes and forward when climbing.

We must have been slowly climbing because it got steadily colder. The rain became heavier. The horses' backs began to steam. I was grateful for the heat percolating through from Bugger Me. The gnome stopped to adjust the jerrycans and I wandered off to cast water. We shared a cigarette. Where, I inquired, was Darius?

'Darius?' He pointed back the way we had come, the fingers

fluttering to indicate the distance that divided us. 'Darius is ill.'

'Darius is coming?'

He grunted.

'Darius is not coming?'

An identical sound. I was alone in the forest with no food, a man who could not talk to me and no idea where we were going. But at least he seemed obsessed with a sense of purpose and an urge to get on. He was clearly dissatisfied with the progress we had been making and urged me forward. He adopted a new ploy, following from the rear and – as we rode along – suddenly swiping Bugger Me from behind. The result was as before. Bugger Me would shoot forward in a mad dash, threatening either to unsaddle me or plunge my face into razor-sharp leaves. I shouted and finally managed to poke his horse so that it reared up most satisfactorily. Thereafter, he restricted himself to whispering at Bugger Me in tones of such evil menace that it was every bit as effective.

Hour followed hour. The gnome whispered insidiously in the forest like a heavy breather. The rain came on more heavily. Leeches reached out for us from the trees, gathering around our necks and wrists like tangled jewellery. Blood began to drip from their bites. Travel books tell you to kill leeches with cigarettes. They make excellent cigarette stubbers but it does not kill them. Occasionally, we would glimpse a field through the trees, not rice at this altitude but manioc growing on almost vertical slopes.

The red soil streamed with water, glistening and slimy. I recalled the comforting passages in my mendacious travel book where travellers were recommended to take a gentle stroll through this terrain, carrying a backpack. I pictured myself slithering and sliding up and down these dangerous screes in increasing despair and exhaustion. We came to a village but my hopes of shelter were dashed. It was long abandoned and choked with hairy creeper that swarmed with spiders.

We rode down the main street, once paved with large blocks of stone that had been ripped up and tumbled by the burrowing plants. We picked our way up a giant's staircase with steps some two feet high. Smashed stone rice-mortars littered the ground as after some domestic affray of gigantic proportions.

It would have been nice to eat, but this was far from the gnome's mind. He did not seem even to drink water, so I tried to ignore my own thirst in the pouring rain and soon a throbbing headache merged with the pounding of the horses' hooves. It was at this point that I remembered that despite all the medication I *had* brought, the aspirins had been left behind.

By late afternoon, we emerged high on a ridge with unbroken forest stretching implausibly far in all directions. Mamasa must be back there somewhere but it was totally invisible. Perched like a swimming pool on a hotel roof was a solitary but magnificent rice-field, the plants that implausibly rich green that only rice can produce. To one side stood a fine sturdy house with smoke rising from the back and a smell of roasting coffee. Children waved delightedly from a veranda. It would be good to stand upright again.

The gnome shouted something and rode up to take the lead. Incredibly, we ignored the house and rode straight past to plunge into forest again. One word was understandable, *terlambat,* 'too late'. I was being punished for riding too slowly. I began to hate the gnome.

The last hour added the torment of despair to the rest of the day's sufferings. The rain hissed bitterly through the leaves all around us and it was dark before we arrived at a miserable shack by the wayside.

I have never been faced with the arrival of two complete strangers at nightfall, both liberally caked with mud and blood, who assumed they could simply eat my food and stay at my house. I hope I never shall. I fear I should display myself less hospitable than my host, a young farmer, and his family, who had migrated from the hot coast lured by the prospect of land they could call their own.

It was a modern house of planking with plenty of gaps to allow the wind to whip in and out. Although we were in the forest, no one wasted wood on a fire for anything but cooking so we sat on the hard floor in our soaked clothes and shivered. It was the moment to dig out my new Mamasa cloak. Though soaked, it would at least keep out the draughts. I buried myself in its clammy folds.

The farmer spoke Indonesian. He had lived here for three years, having been encouraged to migrate by the government. But life was hard. They no longer received any help from the authorities and the first priority was, of course, to get the mosque finished. In the cold up here, you could not get more than one harvest of rice a year whatever you did. Had I heard of the other group of tourists in the mountains? There were four Frenchmen on horses riding about. Darkness fell, but there was no money for an oil lamp. We sat in the dark, our faces only intermittently illuminated by the glow of cigarettes. Children crept in, swathed in thin cloaks. Not for the first time, I felt desperately inadequate. I wished I could play the flute or crack jokes in the language they were whispering in.

Food was brought in, chicken – wealth indeed for a farmer such as this. I too would be grateful for it – not like on Aeroflot. It smelt delicious but suddenly I was too tired to eat. When I tried, my teeth simply could not get into it. I hid it in my cloak for disposal next day. The gnome and the farmer demolished the rest with a great heap of rice. I recalled the restaurant in Ujung Pandang where I had been served a huge colander of rice as 'rice for one person'.

A small child came in and, without formality, sat on my lap. In the obscurity, I passed it the chicken and it chewed in the darkness in conspiratorial silence.

The next thing I knew it was daylight. As a guest I had been guilty of lack of conversation and appetite. To this was to be added the offence of falling asleep in mid-meal. Every limb seemed set in bitter cramp and my mouth was haunted by the familiar furry taste of the overnight Channel crossing. The headache was gone but there was a new problem. I was blind. I could distinguish light from dark but objects had only the vaguest, blurred outlines. My eyes were hot and swollen and someone was driving a hot needle into both irises. There was something wrong with my breathing too. Snot streamed from my nose and I began a sneezing fit that seemed endless and left me weak and gasping. It must be pneumonia. As I lay helpless and terrified a figure swam into view. From the voice, it was the farmer. He was laughing, actually laughing at my suffering. In that moment I knew he had poisoned me. Rage and self-pity fought for mastery and self-pity won. He reached forward and took my cloak. He could not even wait for me to die before stripping the corpse! I was too weak to resist. He giggled again.

'Chilli!' he said.

'What?'

'Chilli. They use chilli to dye the cloth. You should never wear a Mamasa cloth that has not been washed at least three times or better still buy the new ones that don't use plant colours. There is a new smooth sort.' I knew he meant rayon.

He took the cloth away and laughed a good healthy laugh. An hour later, I had washed and eaten some baked manioc. I could see and breathe again and felt the light-hearted relief that recovery from an illness always brings. Only the gnome looked displeased.

He metaphorically, and the horses literally, were champing at the bit. I was no longer capable of leaping on Bugger Me but hauled myself on to the firewood raft of saddle. In my gratitude and relief, I probably gave the farmer too much money. In farewell, he gave the horse a slap. It plunged crazily forward. Another day had begun.

It is hard to distinguish the next four days from one another. They assumed a separate ghostly reality characterized only by the pounding of horses' hooves both inside and outside my head. Sometimes it rained and I was very wet. Sometimes it was sunny and I was very hot. The horses too seemed to become increasingly fractious and fights among them broke out until it became a major inconvenience.

The gnome refused to stop anywhere, being obsessed by some grim and uncertain purpose. I found no Torajans living lives of noble ethnographic simplicity. Indeed, as we moved deeper into the forest, it became denser and less marked by human settlement until there were hardly any people at all. Only occasionally would we come across lonely woodcutters, like as not crouched in wretched, leaky shelters by the roadside or sawing logs into planks by hand. There can be few more miserable roles in life than the bottom half of a two-man saw in a forest in the rain. All the sawdust goes full in your face. But I could not talk to these people. I think the gnome could not either. We must have crossed some invisible linguistic frontier. So we lapsed into total silence except for Bugger Me who still received whispered menaces from the gnome. On occasion we spent the night in one of these shelters in a miasma of sawdust, smoke and mosquitoes, sleep made fitful by the rustling of tin-cans that had been arranged in an elaborate pest-scaring device operated by a string tied to the big toe of the woodcutter in residence. We subsisted on a diet of rice and chilli. I had almost stopped eating.

On the last day, I could tell something was in the air. Our solitude was abruptly shattered by the arrival of a convoy of horses coming the other way. Our own path proved to be the tributary of some greater highway. A deep groove had been worn in the centre of the track by generations of horsemen. All branches above head height had been knocked down by the constant traffic. Unfortunately, I extended rather further in both directions than most of the locals so I was forced to raise my feet to clear the sides of the groove while simultaneously ducking my head to avoid the branches. This, together with the constant danger of a fight amongst the horses, made for a trying journey.

Indonesians drive on the left. This meant that as we climbed the mountain clockwise, we were on the outside, ill-equipped to encounter the descending convoy, its horses splayed out with jerrycans of paraffin so that they knocked and banged against our own, threatening to push us over the edge. There was much dithering and shouting, horses skidding on the loose rock. Feeling that cowardice was the better part of discretion. I abandoned my own mount and climbed on foot. At the top was a middle-aged man in a bright cloak who giggled on seeing me and jumped up and down on the spot in glee.

'*Belanda* – Dutchman!' he cried, pointing at me.

Toraja!' I countered, pointing back. It was the funniest thing he had ever heard and he repeated his little dance of delight. After days of total silence, conversation was heady stuff.

'I thought you were the group of Frenchmen riding through the hills – eight Frenchmen on horseback. But you are alone. Or did the others die?' That seemed funny too.

'Where are you from?' I asked, getting in first.

He pointed over one shoulder. 'From the north.'

'What is in the north?'

'Two kilometres up there is a fine house, then the town.'

We chattered on until the gnome came up, driving the horses before him. My new friend creased his brow.

'One thing I do not understand.' He indicated the horses. 'Why do you travel with two stallions and one mare in heat. Does it not make things difficult?' Clearly, I should have looked at more than the hooves.

Experience had taught me not to take estimates of distance literally. It would be splendid to see what the carved houses of this area looked like. Whatever the gnome said, I would insist on stopping. I got my camera out.

Almost exactly two kilometres later, however, we emerged from the forest. The gnome reigned in his horses, extended a hand in a sort of 'there you are' gesture and uttered his first Indonesian for days. 'We have arrived,' he announced with all the decorum of a footman.

We were standing in the centre of an immaculate putting-green, whose tender surface looked as though it would be bruised by an unkind word. Staring at us in some dismay were a group of Japanese, faultlessly attired in what must be deemed 'leisure wear', shorts and checked shirts, gesturing with ergonomic putting-irons that we should ride around rather than across their golf course. They seemed in no way surprised by our appearance and as we circuited the fringe of grass under the trees, they returned to their practice, peaked American baseball caps purposefully bent towards the balls they addressed.

The fine house was not, as I had assumed, an ancient carved dwelling. It was an American-style bungalow, with shiny aluminium roof and plastic floor-tiles. Most important, however, to one bereft of food and drink, it was clearly some sort of clubhouse or at least a bar. I felt a brief absurd moment of panic that I would not be allowed in without a tie.

There is always pleasure in re-enacting, in the flesh, the cliches of the cinema. We climbed stiffly down, beating the dust from our clothes as Roy Rogers was wont to do and hitched our horses to the rail in front of the building. We sauntered, stiff-legged as John Wayne, into the building and went up to the bar. My camera hung about my neck like an accusation.

I did not expect to be understood but somehow had to say it.

'Gimme coupla beers.' The barman flashed a grin.

'Sure boss. You want Japanese or domestic?'

'Domestic. You speak good English.'

'Sure. I had three years in the nickel mines up north with the Canadians. I speak but good. You with the group of Frenchmen on horseback – twelve of them with three guides?'

'No. What is this place?'

'This coffee plantation. All the Japanese managers come here from outstations. Coffee cooked here. Where you from? You got kinda funny accent.'

'From Mamasa. We came over the mountains by horse.'

'You crazy. Why you don't come by truck like everyone else?'

'By truck?' As if on cue, a truck could be heard reversing outside.

'Oh.' The gnome was sucking down beer, making interrogative gestures about further supplies. I felt I ought to get angry if only I could be bothered.

'Are all the people who come here Japanese?'

'We got some guys work up at the radio station. They spend all their time watching porno movies over the satellite from Thailand, so they don't come in much.'

On the wall above his head was a carefully lettered sign in English defining the Rules of the Club.

'The palm-trees to the west of the green are to accounted a natural hazard as are the dropping of animals.'

'Is there anywhere to stay?'

'Sure. There's a joint down the main street.'

I led Bugger Me down the road, a line of makeshift houses with a frontier air about them. No one seemed to be dropping animals.

The 'joint' was readily identifiable by the stack of beer bottles and the line of sheets hanging on the fence. The gnome and I terminated our arrangement with the passing of money. When I removed the large roll of raddled notes from my pocket, there was a leech nestling in the centre like a symbol of usury.

The establishment was run by a depressed-looking Chinese whose growing family had expanded into virtually all the rooms, thus simultaneously increasing his expenditure and cutting his income.

The latest addition was a bony son who had returned from studying architecture and lived on a balcony producing drawings of skyscrapers that would never be built. He had a very loud cassette-player on which he listened to pop-music and Christian sermons with equal enjoyment.

There was not much room for me, so to minimize my disruption of domestic arrangements I was allocated part of the floor in a room that otherwise contained the giggling pubescent daughters of the house. They were shielded from my impudent gaze by the curtains that surrounded their four-poster bed. A constant stream pattered in and out so that I never quite knew how many were inside as the curtains danced and bulged to whatever female operations were carried out there.

These distractions were as nothing to those of the clock whose electronic chimes produced a sound, on the hour, similar *to* that produced by British battleships. When I mentioned it to the owner, he swelled with pride.

'My son did that,' he said. 'Before it was very quiet.'

Despairing of sleep, I went to find the gnome. He had already filled his jerrycans with paraffin and immediately set off back to Mamasa. As for me, I thought I might as well use that motor road and go on to Rantepao.

OF RICE AND MEN

The first thing I saw as the truck pulled into Rantepao was a mosque painted a prosperous green and adorned with a dome beaten from aluminium sheeting. It was the fasting month and till dusk no Muslims would be eating or drinking. A pious mumble came from inside. The second thing was a man bent double outside the mosque vomiting copiously. He was clearly drunk and promising whatever God it was he served a better life in future. My fellow-passengers tutted censoriously. Not a Torajan, they assured me. On the dashboard was a sticker, 'Christ died for your sins.' Two ancillary images of scantily clad Chinese girls and a man drinking stout suggested what those sins might have been.

After the horse-ride from Mamasa, I felt cosmically fractious – simultaneously cold and hungry and tired and bored with no notion of what it might be that could reinstitute a state of well-being.

Near the market was a small hotel. Small, clean and inexpensive, it seemed it might offer solace for spiritual outrage. In the centre of the garden stood a Torajan rice-barn. These beautiful structures are to be seen all over the mountainsides. They stand some twenty-five feet high on great tubular legs and are richly carved and painted all over. The crowning glory is the roof, a gracefully concave curve of bamboo tiles that sticks out fore and aft like an admiral's hat. Underneath is the platform, that most important social space in a Torajan village. It is always cool under the barn. There is always a convenient surface to lean your back against. I slipped off my shoes and settled back to doze.

We never know what fate has in store, at what point blind chance will enter into our lives in a way that we will afterwards re-gloss as due to our own intentions and planning. As I sat, psychologically and physically outraged, on the platform of a rice-barn in the middle of Indonesia, fate decided to send me something I was not even looking for – a field-work assistant. He came not in a puff of smoke but in a waiter's uniform.

'Hallo boss!' I opened grudging eyes to see a small dark figure, grinning from ear to ear and tossing a tray up in the air to catch it again on the outspread fingers of one hand. He dropped it with a clatter.

'I bring you a beer?'

'Yes, all right.' He walked away whistling a sickly pop-song and kicking the tray as he went. He returned with a beer that he opened with an exaggerated flick of the wrist so that the top was propelled into the air to be caught deftly on the way down. The bottle was plopped down and he slid on to the rice-barn.

'You got a smoke boss?' I produced a cigarette.

'Where are you from? My name's Johannis.' We started on the usual litany of questions and answers. Another waiter emerged yawning and scratching as though from a ten years' sleep and sat down on the barn. Soon the cook joined us.

'The boss is away today,' they announced and eyed the beer. Soon we were all playing cards – a game rather like dominoes – and sharing the beer. A child entered on a ramshackle bicycle, was swiftly plucked off it and sat on a lap.

'My cousin,' explained the cook. A fat man – a neighbour – shuffled in to read the newspaper. He was the driver of a very wealthy Christian lady who had made Christian pilgrimages to the Holy Land fashionable. He speculated lavishly on her private life.

'Let's get some palm-wine,' said a figure at the back. It was the boss's son, clearly throwing in his lot with the reprobates. Soon foaming bamboo tubes of the brew were standing around. Johannis fussily insisted on transferring the contents to an enamel teapot before pouring it into glasses.

I received an impromptu introduction to the various kinds of wine. We tried highland and lowland, the sort with red tree bark, fresh and day-old. It was an excellent frothy brew. It is perhaps the strongest argument yet advanced for the existence of a benevolent deity that you can prod a palm-tree with a knife and extract a wholesome and heady brew, palm-wine, as sap. The sugar of the sap is fermented by natural yeasts. The older the brew, the less sugar, the more alcohol. Unless tampered with, it is extremely pure, having been filtered through the entire length of the tree-trunk. Its only disadvantage is a strong laxative effect.

'You like?' I liked and was rewarded with slaps and hugs. The conversation took a more philosophical turn. Indonesian television finds Britain a source of much cheap copy so people tend to have views on the country. Mrs Thatcher was discussed at length and found to be good because strong. In Indonesian politics strength is good in itself regardless of the ends to which it is put. Also, she was beautiful. Curiously, even here the British royal family was a focus of attention. The recent marriage of Prince Andrew had been much appreciated though enthusiasm had outstripped comprehension. It was widely believed that the male character involved was Prince Charles who had taken a second wife and must therefore have converted to Islam. But now the devil seemed to have us all firmly by the neck.

'Let's go cock-fighting. Puttymen like cock-fighting?'

'In the old days,' explained Johannis, 'this was more than just an entertainment. If you had a problem with someone and needed to decide the quarrel between you, you could use the fighting cocks.'

We were led behind some houses and across a yard. The cook seemed to be having difficulty walking. Ducking under some washing, we came out in a large cleared space containing some fifty men and boys all looking about furtively. Someone came up and remonstrated with Johannis.

'They were not happy to have a tourist here. It is illegal. But I explained you were a friend. Anyway, that man is a policeman.'

People broke up into little knots and conversation intensified. Money was waved around. Someone began to shout and collect cash in a straw hat. Two huge, glossy cockerels were whipped out from under sarongs and preened relentlessly. Vicious steel spurs were attached to their dew-claws and the owners prodded and poked the birds at each other to excite their hostility. These seemed, however, to be particularly pacific beasts, far less aggressive than Torajan horses. They cooed at each other and rubbed necks adoringly. It does not take much anthropological or even popular Freudian flair to see an association between the virility of the cock and that of its owner. Torajans clearly made the same association. Sniggering broke out and the owners began to blush, their faces turning a deeper brown. Johannis slung an arm around my neck and giggled, holding his little finger out and drooping it suggestively. One of the owners broke into a heavy sweat and began to slap the black bird. Suddenly, it squawked and shot into the air. There was a brief, inconclusive flurry of feathers as if both birds were trying to get into the air but were too heavily laden. Blood seeped through the chest feathers of its opponent and it slumped over. The black bird stamped exultantly on the corpse of its defeated rival. It lay inert and broken like a limp bundle of rags. An object of pride had become an embarrassment.

Squabbling now broke out among the men, shouting and waving of fists. The man with the straw hat plumped it back on his head, money and all, and stood rock-like and grim, his arms folded across his chest.

'They want their money back,' explained Johannis.

'But why?'

'That man shoved a broken chilli up his bird's bum.'

'Oh. I see.'

The policeman emerged from the crowd and began a pantomime of moderation, fluttering fingers raised in supplication as though beating down flames.

'Now *he* wants the money,' said Johannis delightedly. 'Can you imagine anyone trusting a policeman with money?'

The victor seized washing from the line and began to gesticulate dramatically with a tablecloth.

'He wants the leg of the dead chicken. It's his right.'

The owner of the defeated chicken grabbed its corpse by a leg and brandished it in his opponent's face.

'Now he wants to be paid for *his* chicken.'

A woman emerged and began shouting louder than them all.

'What does she want? Did she have a bet?'

'No. It's her tablecloth.'

Rantepao offers little to those in search of nightlife. Most houses are clapped up and firmly shuttered by eight o'clock. The market contains the odd late reveller buying soap or cooking oil. Occasionally, the cinema offers attractions such as *Wallowing in Mud,* a very mildly erotic story of 'night butterflies'. Apart from this, there is only the crossroads as a focus of nocturnal activity. Here, people come and sit blankly, wrapped in their cloaks, and gaze at the empty streets. Trishaw drivers doze in their seats and banter with each other, all buses having ceased their raucous clamour for passengers at nightfall – about six o'clock.

One or two street lamps cast a feeble pall and illuminate piles of vegetable rubbish left over from the day's trading. Dogs root in them with a desperate optimism. Groups of schoolchildren cluster under the lights like moths – no *not* like moths – boys in one group, girls in another, eyeing each other with the excitement that comes from mutual ignorance.

As I passed later that evening, a lone figure in the flimsy shirt of a high-school student detached itself from a group and hailed me.

'Hallo, boss. Where you go?'

'Johannis! Why are you in a school uniform?' It was always hard to place the ages of Indonesians. Surely he was too old to be still at school?

He waved a book at me. *Introduction to Biology.* There's no electricity at my house and they complain if I burn paraffin just to read, so we have to come here and study under the street lamps.' A wave of post-imperial guilt struck me. I thought of my own world of bedside lamps, scholarships and libraries.

'You are still at school?'

He sighed. 'I should be married but, yes, I am still at school. I have to keep stopping my studies to go back and work in the rice-fields. Or I work at hotels to get the money for school fees. It takes so long. One more year and I can finish. Then I can look for a job.'

'What sort of job?' He looked at me as if I were mad.

'*Any* job. My parents are getting too old to work in the fields. We sons must help.'

'Do you work tomorrow?'

'No. Tomorrow I go to a funeral.' He seemed visibly cheered at the prospect. 'Hey, why don't you come too?'

'A funeral? Wouldn't people mind?'

He laughed. 'No. The more visitors, the more honour. We go

together. I don't want to go to the hotel. I might see the boss. You come here tomorrow at eight. We find a truck together. It's polite to wear something black.'

I was wakened by the sound of cockerels. My sins were coming home to roost. A muffled yelling and slamming of doors suggested that the boss had returned and that our debauch of the previous day had not gone undetected. An atmosphere of sultry guilt, of walking on eggs, hung over the establishment. I slid out without breakfast.

Johannis was wearing a black T-shirt with the legend, 'Born to be a Winner' and a pair of jeans labelled 'Bing Crosby'. The only black shirt I had was one from the Thai family-planning campaign, showing condoms in the poses of the three wise monkeys. Johannis assured me it would do fine. The government was pushing family planning. They would think I was a big Bapak from a ministry.

Torajan funerals are inherently jolly occasions, at least in the later stages, for grief is long behind them. The body may well have been kept for several years while resources are mobilized and people summoned from abroad. Migration abroad has long been a response to the harshness of life in the mountains. But Torajans always come back – especially for festivals such as this.

It was only a small event by local standards. Some funerals cost hundreds of thousands of dollars and are visited by ambassadors and cabinet ministers. This was a local affair. It would be family, friends, neighbours. The truck dropped us off at the end of the tarmac road. There was a walk of several miles up slippery tracks whose churned-up surface was a testament to the popularity of the event. I struggled and slid in my shoes. Johannis grinned and slid off his flip-flops, gripping the earth with splayed, horny toes.

We fell in with a group of other people labouring up the hill with burdens that I knew I could never manage, long bamboo tubes of palm-wine overflowing gently with froth, two men with pigs, converted with rattan loops into handbags that they tucked under their arms. Six men laboured under the burden of a huge sow whose belly dragged along the ground, so that it squealed and struggled. All were laughing and shouting.

'They will get to eat meat,' explained Johannis. 'In Toraja, it's rare to eat meat. Often, we have to make do with rice and chilli.' I thought of those mournful meals on the road from Mamasa.

From afar, came the sound of a gong and an abrupt and incongruous cheer. Rounding a corner, we gained a broad view across the valley to the festival site. Immediately the whole convoy came to a halt. A large two-storeyed barn had been erected, looking rather like a film set. It overshadowed the traditional houses, gleaming with modern gloss paint in the sunlight. Long cloths fluttered from poles, snaking out over a crowd that seethed and boiled around the house stilts. Wood-smoke hung heavy in the air. Across from the houses were the rice-barns, weighed down under the throngs of visitors.

'Wah!' Johannis pointed in excitement. 'A bullfight.'

It was not what we think of as a bullfight, a heavily armed man against domesticated cattle. It was two enormous water buffaloes pitted against each other, huffing and puffing like Sumo wrestlers. Their owners had led their ponderous charges on leads attached to rings through their noses. Their horns were adorned with red streamers. As with the cockerels, the secret was to push and prod them at each other until they lost their tempers, locked horns and fought. The owners had to dodge out of the way without looking as if they were doing more than stepping casually to one side. There came a mighty crash as the heads smashed into each other, horn on horn and bone on bone. The crowd roared. The horns shoved and twisted. The larger of the two suddenly broke and fled like a distressed matron, scattering a chaff of little boys before it.

To their delight its owner, decked in all his finery, fell headlong in the mud and the charging buffalo was turned by an urchin who threw clods of dirt at it. The man picked himself up and looked into his beast's eyes in reproach.

'You see,' said Johannis puffing out his chest, 'one is big but the little one is brave and tough. Just like you and me!' He slapped me on the back and laughed.

We had arrived in good time. Raddled, hung-over faces bleared at us from every doorway. Children wandered forlornly between the structures carrying food. Hawking, throat-and nostril-clearing noises came from all directions. Children waved and called, 'Hallo mister!'

Johannis asked directions and we were pointed to one of the houses. After much interrogation from above, a wrinkled little old man descended the steep ladder. To come downstairs elegantly in a long skirt is apparently an exercise set for débutantes. This man was a master of the art. He raised his black sarong with one hand and came down face-forward, somehow gripping the ladder with his heels. I produced a pack of cigarettes from my bag and they vanished inside the folds of his attire. 'Number fifteen!' he said. All the buildings were numbered.

The occupants of number fifteen were a cheery bunch, vaguely related to Johannis. They had already begun drinking palm-wine and the woven walls had absorbed the agreeable smell of clove cigarettes and marks of previous roistering. They fell into a long conversation in the course of which Johannis became increasingly quiet and began to blush. As he became quieter, the others laughed more and more. A group of old ladies in the corner muttered and hid their noses. Johannis refused to say what the conversation was about.

His friends, however, were eager to translate and increase his discomfiture.

'It is a matter of bamboo,' they explained, nudging each other. Bamboo?

'Yes. You see at festivals like this that last for several days, we have the chance to meet girls after dark – people from far away. Sometimes, if they are willing, they meet us apart. Johannis met a girl last time in the bamboo clump. But bamboo makes you itch – you know. You have to scratch your skin. The girl's mother found marks on her daughter's back and beat her.' He clapped his hands. 'It was wonderful! How she cried! But she was clever. She didn't tell Johannis's name. All she would say is that she had been there to smell the flowers.' To smell the flowers?

'Yes,' said Johannis miserably. 'My family name is *Bunga,* "flower". To smell the flowers, to kiss Bunga – it is the same in our language.' He looked lovelorn and suddenly very small.

A little child appeared at the bottom of the ladder and beamed up at us. Johannis looked angry and swatted at him. In his hand, the waif held the genitals of a bull killed the day before. By inserting his fingers at strategic points, he was able to produce a sudden and alarming erection to be waved in the faces of guests.

'Come,' said Johannis determinedly. 'We shall go and see the body.'

It appeared that the deceased was female and had been kept in the house for nearly four years following her death, the juices of putrefaction being absorbed by copious wrappings. There was certainly no disagreeable odour emanating from the large bundle that contained the cadaver.

'Nowadays they cheat,' said Johannis, 'with formalin from the hospital.'

The body was stored in the front room of the house, the walls being swathed with rich cloths and patchwork quilts. The outer covering of the corpse was bright red, the same shade exactly as the child's tricycle parked beside it. Johannis ignored the body.

'That's a fine tricycle,' he said. 'Look.' He pushed a switch and it began to emit a police siren and flash red and blue lights. 'Wah!'

A man leant against the body, smoking. He got up from time to time and swatted at a gong. It was the sound we had heard from across the valley. 'Not just anyone is allowed to do that you know,' he said with the sense of power of a car-park attendant.

It is hard to know what to do when being shown a body. Admiration seems inappropriate. Should one comment on the size of it? It seemed better to limit myself to vacuous questions of the royal-family-being-shown-industrial-wonder sort. How long? How exactly? Religion of deceased? Polite, slightly impressed concern seemed to be the emotion to display.

A young man entered and reached behind the body, stretching until he was almost lying on top of it to pull forth a cache of cassettes stored there. He dumped them on the body and dug around again for a large black boogie-box. He inserted a Michael Jackson tape and danced off, buttocks gyrating to a blare of saxophones. Cassettes were left spilled along the corpse like a colourful offering. There was a notable absence of awe and piety in the presence of death.

An insistent hammering noise came from the roof. I looked up. It was galvanized iron and rain was falling. In the old days, it would have been the soft patter on bamboo tiles.

'Yes,' he said, 'they're rich people here. The best part is that if you don't have the traditional roof you don't have to spend all that money on ceremonies – killing pigs and such. It leaves money for the children's education.' Clearly, it was a theme of Johannis's life.

From outside came a blaring, barking noise. The portholelike windows were flung open and below could be seen a portly Chinese figure in immaculate shorts, yelling through a portable loudspeaker. The most impressive thing about him was an enormous paunch that seemed more an optional bolt-on fitment than an integral part of his person. Only gradually did it become apparent that he was shouting in French and that behind him trudged twenty or so puttypersons all of whom were complaining loudly. At the rear there were three or four Indonesians who seemed to have nervous tics.

'Wah!' said Johannis with pleasure. 'Tourists!'

They entered the village like an invading army, pushing camera lenses into people's faces, sitting on the rice-barns in their shoes without invitation. They gave nothing but declared loudly that they were not having fun, that they were bored. The Torajans looked at each other in consternation and arranged to give them coffee. Most rejected it. Then rice was offered.

'We don't eat rice!' a red-faced woman shouted.

Another was trying to buy one of the cloths, grabbing at the textiles on the house front. Through the interpreter it was explained that it was a borrowed heirloom and not for sale. She looked sour and stalked away.

Johannis and I retreated to number fifteen and cowered in the gloom but were detected by the guides. One came and glared furiously at Johannis.

'You have no permit. Why are you working as a guide?'

'I'm a Torajan,' snapped back Johannis. 'Where are you from – Bali?'

'It's like this,' I intervened, 'this man's not my guide, he's my friend.' There was a stunned silence. It felt a ridiculous thing to say – absurdly explicit – something that should be expressed in gesture or left implicit. Yet as I said it, I knew it was true. I had at one time lived for some eighteen months in an African village yet not met a single person I would call a friend. Yet here, the making of friends seemed almost inevitable. Was it some unconscious bias against Africa? It seemed unlikely. Was it simply that in that area of Africa there was no notion of friendship that corresponded to our own? A man's friends were inevitably drawn from those he was circumcised with. There was no provision in their culture for meeting people you were not related to and feeling mutual affinity and sympathy. In Torajaland the ties of family were strong, indeed unbreakable, for they extended beyond the grave. Yet there was room for friendships too. Was it simply that in that part of Africa people tended to approach you either with embarrassing servility or arrogant hostility, whereas a Torajan farmer would look you straight in the eye and talk to you as an equal? Maybe it was simply the different cultural expectations aroused by a white face – a different history of colonialism. Whatever it was, it felt very real.

There was a deafening crashing of gongs. A French child had penetrated the house and was inflicting many years' wear on the aged instrument in a few short minutes. Rain started again in thick, heavy drops but guests were still arriving in dribs and drabs as well as more formal delegations. In the latter case, they formed up outside the village and, after much preliminary preening, were accosted by men dressed as warriors, wearing horned helmets and waving spears. Emitting yodelled whoops and yelps, they confronted the visitors and conducted them to make their offerings and take their seats. The more progressive visitors had bought matching T-shirts with the name of their hamlet stamped on the front. Pigs, the small change of ritual obligation, were lugged in in a rough and ready fashion, while buffalo were paraded with great style. Elegant ladies glided about with areca-nut and coffee. A man with a school notebook came up and recorded the offerings. He nodded agreeably.

'When there is a festival in *their* village, we will give these things back,' he explained to me.

'Do only people from other villages give?'

'No. Everyone gives. Friends give. Children give. They must give buffalo if they want to inherit rice-fields. No buffalo, no fields.'

'What did they give from your village, Johannis?'

'Oh well. We are not so close. Anyway, we have no buffalo left. My brother just graduated from the university in Ujung Pandang. That cost fifteen buffalo. If it were not for the coffee crop, I would not get to school at all.'

A resonant pounding wafted out from behind one of the houses.

'Ah. You will want to see this.' He led me over. Women were gathered around an empty rice-mortar, a huge hollowed-out tree-trunk, their black clothes fluttering as they pounded away. To the instructions of a stern lady, they were beating a rapid rhythm on the wood with heavy pestles.

Torajan festivals are rigorously divided between those of the east and life and those of the west and death. Rice is strongly associated with life and so close relatives must give up rice when they are in mourning. The empty rice-mortar proclaimed this self-denial to the world. Ironically, it also acted as a sort of dinner gong. Ladies began carrying meat and rice into the shelters or teetered around under buckets of syrupy coffee. In honour of the occasion, rice was heaped up in the middle of the floor in a glistening red heap.

'Boiled with blood,' announced the guide in French to the tourists next door. There were Gallic cries of disgust. I translated for Johannis.

'He is wrong. It just grows red.'

'The blood of pigs and buffalo, sometimes dogs,' continued the voice authoritatively. Those few French who had tasted any rice could now be heard retching ... 'It is allowed to clot overnight before being scooped up and roasted.' A female voice could be heard saying, 'No,' feebly.

'They slit the throats of the animals and catch it all hot in long bamboo tubes ...'

A male voice said in French, 'I've been looking at this palm-wine. It looks a little pink. You don't suppose ...'

Johannis proffered a dish of buffalo meat and pig fat. It was very tough. I settled for a boiled egg up one end of the platter. A ravishingly beautiful girl with long, black hair and flawless golden skin came to clear away the dish.

Johannis gawped. 'I will help her.'

I did not see him for the next hour and a half, but he kindly came and fetched me down to the field where stone monoliths stood like miniature henges.

'Come. They will kill a buffalo.'

A man with long hair tied up in a headband led in a buffalo, dancing and tossing its head. There was a long and inexplicable delay of the sort that precedes events the world over. The French reappeared fluttering and complaining. They pointed at me.

'See. *He* was here first. Ah, these guides.'

The man with the notebook came and inspected the buffalo like an accountant. He checked the notebook and began a long interrogation of the man who had brought in the beast. Finally, it was led away.

'Zut, alors. Merde.'

After an interminable delay, two smaller buffalo were brought back and tethered to stakes by the foot. The accountant fussed around taking notes. Mischievous-looking children came up, leaning on pointed bamboo tubes. The child with the portable erection displayed it with simple pride to the French ladies.

'Aah. Disgusting! It looks like you, Jean.'

An aged gentleman, bent under the weight of years,

approached and began a very long, very slow oration.

'A *to minaa,* a high priest of the old religion ...' explained the guide.

Johannis snorted. 'He's just the head of the house.'

The French fussed with exposures and angles.

'... A chant unchanged for thousands of years ...' said the guide.

'He's explaining that he's a Christian so he won't eat any of this meat,' corrected Johannis.

'... Telling a myth about the old days ...' said the guide.

'... and the Blessed Virgin Mary,' ended the old man.

The man with the headband pulled a wickedly sharp machete from its sheath. Holding the rope that tethered the buffalo, he stroked it almost caressingly across its throat. A silence. A red line appeared across the beast's neck. Then it began to gasp and roll its eyes as a fountain of gore shot out. The little boys strained forward, the slayer keeping them back with an outstretched arm as the buffalo staggered and stumbled. Finally, it coughed and tumbled to its knees. The children dashed into the ebbing fountain of blood thrusting sharp bamboo tubes, giggling, into the gaping wound to collect the hot blood. Their hands and faces streamed with it. It matted their hair and washed into their eyes. They staggered away with their slopping tubes, jostling their elders who were stripping the skin from the still twitching corpse and tumbling its steaming guts on to the grass.

The second buffalo was straining to escape, but the man with the headband walked straight up and slashed it across the throat. As before, there was a gush of blood and the little boys had to be restrained. But this time, the beast did not fall. Instead, it broke free and dashed up the hill to the festival pursued by men waving swords. The crowd above squealed and broke before it – the men fearing for their lives, the women for their clothes. Finally, it was cornered and calmed. The slaughterer slashed it again. Once more it pulled free, spraying blood in all directions. Twice more they tried to kill it. Only gradually did a slow twitching spread from its feet through,the whole body and it fell. There were sighs of relief from the crowd. Johannis chuckled.

'Magic. Someone is trying to spoil the festival.' He pursed his lips and nodded sagely. The little boys looked annoyed. There was not a drop of blood left in the creature. The French were anxiously clicking away, 'Terrible, awful,' as the guide spewed forth endless commentary.

'Enough, now,' said Johannis. 'We go back to town.'

An enterprising contractor had laid on an *ad hoc* bus service back to Rantepao. He laughed as I climbed on.

'Look out. There is a giant getting in.' He began collecting fares, red hundred-rupiah notes fanned between his fingers.

'Hang on,' cried a matronly lady as he took mine. 'Why are you charging him more?'

The driver immediately switched to Torajan, Johannis delightedly translating: 'I charge him more because he is bigger.' 'Yes, but he has no luggage. Anyway, I will sit on his lap.' 'It is up to me how much I charge him.' 'Yes, but the price to charter this bus is fifteen thousand. If you charge him more, I will pay less.'

The driver returned and pressed money in my hand. He grinned. 'Puttyman's reduction.'

Johannis chuckled, put his arms behind his head and executed one of those vicious spine-wrenching twists that Indonesians consider to be good for their backs.

'Tomorrow,' he said dreamily, 'I am going back to my village, Baruppu'. Why don't you come too?'

'Why not? Thank you, Johannis.'

At the bus station was one of those awkward moments where relationships are defined for all time. I reached in my pocket.

'Er … Johannis …'

He backed away. 'Look. You are a rich man. I am very poor. So when you leave you give me something. Maybe your shoes.' He looked at my very large, very disreputable shoes. 'Well, maybe not your shoes but something *like* your shoes. But don't give me money. It would be insulting.' A friend, then.

'I meet you tomorrow. Now I go eat at my uncle's house. Then, maybe I go back to the festival.'

'To look at the bamboo?'

He grinned. 'Yes, maybe I look at the bamboo. In that village is some very fine bamboo.'

At the hotel, the proprietor was all smiles. Either my part in yesterday's debauch was unknown or it was pardoned on the grounds that all kinds of anti-social behaviour are expected of a guest. But it was not to be a peaceful night. There was a nervous plucking at my sleeve and I turned to see a small, ferrety man with nervous, darting eyes.

'Hallo, boss. I am Hitler. Maybe you have heard of me.' It was hard to know what to say to that. Maybe I had misheard.

'Hitler?'

'Yes, Pak, my father used to hear the name on the radio before I was born and liked it.'

He pulled me to my door and in the light of the dim bulb pushed a Polaroid picture at me. Another hairy-legged transvestite? No. It was a wooden grave-figure, the sort of thing Torajans have in front of their tombs, rather a good one.

'You buy, Pak? I hear you from a museum.'

'No. You know I'm not allowed to buy old things. I'm not looking for trouble.'

'I get it to Bali for you. From Bali, you can get it anywhere. Everybody does it. I got a friend.' He mentioned the name of a London dealer.

'No.'

He switched tactics. 'This is not an old grave-figure. Just a very good one. I give you a good price.' It took time to disengage myself without rudeness but finally it was done and I was sinking into oblivion. There was a firm knocking at the door. Another man. He looked outraged.

'My brother came to see you.'

'Your brother?'

'Hitler.'

'Oh God.'

'Why don't you want to buy from him? You get a better offer?'

'No. I just want to go to sleep.' I tried pushing the door. He pushed it back.

'A coffin – an old, carved coffin. You buy?'

'No!' Finally the door was shut but it seemed only minutes before there was a knocking again. Broad sunlight streamed through the window. I opened the door. A fat hand pushed me back into the room.

'You know me?' the voice hissed. It was the policeman from the cock-fight.

'Yes, I know you.'

'Good. There is a man outside. His name is Hitler. He is a dealer in stolen property. He will try to sell you a grave-figure. Whatever the price he asks, say you will take it. You will be helping the Indonesian Republic. I want to arrest him.'

'Now look. Not so fast ...' Someone was clearly being set up here but how could I be sure it was not me? A rich tourist. Someone who worked for a museum. I looked a pretty good suspect in my own eyes.

'Just agree to everything,' hissed the policeman. Why was he whispering? 'I should hate to think you were not a friend of the

Republic. Your name will not be mentioned.'

Without waiting for an answer, he opened the door and dragged Hitler in. Hitler extolled the virtues of the figure, its age, the simplicity of its lines. The policeman poked me in the ribs from time to time and nodded enthusiastically at me. I was determined not to agree to buy it. Yet at the same time, the air was heavy with menace. What was to stop them simply cooking up a story between them? I clearly could not turn them down flat either.

'You will appreciate,' I began, 'that I have to be very careful. It is a very beautiful grave-figure.' The policeman smiled. 'But it might be illegal for me to buy it.' He poked me and scowled. 'I shall have to see the figure. I could not buy something I had not seen.' Both now looked worried. 'Perhaps we could meet at another time in another place.' The two looked at each other.

'Perhaps,' said Hitler, 'I could bring it here tonight?'

'Good idea!' By tonight I would be in Johannis's village. The policeman poked me again. 'I am sure you can buy it now.'

'No. I absolutely must see it first before I buy.' He brightened.

'You buy? Right, we come back tonight.'

They walked back to their motorbike. As they left, the policeman gave me a horrible wink.

Proprietors of buses did not risk their newest stock on the Baruppu' route. Our bus was hideously scarred and pocked. It had clearly gone through a period when cosmetic attempts had been made upon its virtue but such times were now long behind it. It was frowsy and broken down and it knew it. Johannis eyed the occupants appraisingly.

'Too much *cewek*. Not enough men.'

It seemed an odd remark for him to make.

'When we get stuck,' he explained, 'the women and pigs stay inside. Only the men get out and push.' Pigs? I looked inside. There they lay, trussed with bamboo between their legs.

Johannis had bought meat, eggs, garlic and chilli. It looked like Baruppu' was a famine area. We drove around town several times in the fashion I had now become used to. The driver stopped and ate. One man miraculously withdrew money from the cash desk of the electricity company. Coconuts were pushed under our feet. The vehicle settled ever lower on its springs. A menacingly pregnant woman was embarked. A bicycle was dismantled and stowed behind. Children were parked on laps, luggage shifted to less convenient positions. Everyone smoked and shut the window tightly, although it was a far from cold day.

The instrumentation of the minibus indicated an implausible state of simultaneous emergency on all systems. The brake warning light was on, as was the oil light. We had no petrol or water. The battery was declared to be discharging continuously. At every source of water, the driver would halt and pour gallons on to and beside the passenger seat. This was not the position of the radiator but of the clutch, which grew so hot that the front passenger's plastic sandals began to smoulder.

Fares were collected. It was explained that this was so that the driver would have enough money to buy petrol. Finally, we stopped at the petrol station. The attendant pointed at me, 'Turiis!' he declared with a grin.

The bus company clearly had some link with this establishment, for the attendant threw off his peaked cap like a mark of servitude, sprang into the driver's seat, revved the engine and shot off with a yodelled whoop. Only I seemed surprised.

'Wah!' cried Johannis with a pure delight that made me feel old and jaded. The other men beat their thighs with their hands in exuberance and joined in what I would later recognize as the Torajan war-cry.

Entrance to a Torajan village showing ricefields and traditional houses.

Torajan ricebarns at Nangala.

Top RIGHT Nenek Tulian in priestly dress for a funeral.

CENTRE LEFT Schoolchildren performing on traditional bamboo instruments.

CENTRE RIGHT Men parading in warrior dress.

BOTTTOM A coffin containing the deceased, wrapped in cloth with gold decoration.

TOP LEFT Reopening of the coffin for rewrapping of body and final insertion in tomb.

CENTRE LEFT A sacrificial buffalo being washed in a stream.

CENTRE RIGHT Distribution of buffalo meat to relatives and neighbours.

BOTTTOM Tombs hollowed out of the rockface.

The market at Rantepao.

The start of a cock fight.

The interior of traditional house, Baruppu'.

A woman weaving a cloth, Mamasa.

Constructing the roof, Museum of Mankind, London.

Fitting together the body of the barn.

TOP RIGHT Nenek Tulian carving a panel.

CENTRE LEFT The door of the ricebarn showing a stylised buffalo.

CENTRE RIGHT The façade of the ricebarn showing two cockerels.

BOTTTOM Removal of the scaffolding.

The complete ricebarn, Museum of Mankind, London.

MOUNTAIN
BARNSTORMERS

An early morning mist still hung about the valleys, lurking among the trees and undergrowth. Although it was barely light, one of the great tidal waves of schoolchildren was in full spate. They emerged from the thick bush on either side of the road, hugging their textbooks in anticipation of the duties of matrimony, and picked their way among the rocks that soon replaced any attempt at tarmac.

The bus bucked and heaved up a spiral path until suddenly we broke through the cloud and beneath us lay the boiling cauldron of Rantepao, wreathed in steam with range after range of hillpeaks stretching away as far as the eye and imagination could see. The tops glinted with the first dewy rays of the sun. 'Wah!' cried a voice as if from Heaven, 'Beautiful.' I extended my neck with difficulty out of the window and saw for the first time that the roof had been colonized. Two radiantly happy small children perched atop with the deep joy that deadly peril brings to the truly young.

After about an hour of buttock-wrenching progress, we paused. The driver turned round in his seat and grinned wickedly at me. 'Nyonya Bambang,' he said. It was hard to know what to make of that. The implication from the tone of voice was that this was going to be good. *Nyonya* is the term for a respectable married woman, while Bambang is a man's name. The answer soon became clear.

There emerged from a nearby house a man of offensive cleanliness. He positively gleamed. Once again, I was transported back to school. This was teacher's pet. Before mounting the seat beside the driver – which he assumed as his right – he dusted it off with a spotless handkerchief. He addressed me as being the only person worthy of his attention. 'My name is Bambang. I am an architect from Jakarta.' He extended a hand like a dead fish. Bambang refused my offer of a cigarette. Indeed he insisted the windows be opened to allow the smoke to dissipate. He passed me his visiting card and seemed put out that I had none of my own to offer in exchange. We went through the usual round of questions establishing professional and marital bona fides. He was here to visit relatives, he explained, and to study the traditional architecture of Torajaland. His tragedy was that he loved babies but hated children. The logical result of these principles, twelve children, drove him from the house until he was tempted to sire another one, which gave him a year or two of consolation but ultimately increased his discomfiture. This trip to visit relatives was one of many to escape his prodigious offspring.

The road became abruptly worse, or rather the driver seemed to be aiming for the potholes rather than avoiding them. Bambang began to look green and retch, dabbing at his mouth in a matronly fashion. The driver appeared immensely pleased and puffed smoke aggressively. Most of it went in Bambang's face. Johannis sat quietly, looking out of the window and clutching his groceries to protect them from damage.

'How,' I inquired politely, 'are the eggs?' Everyone screamed with laughter. I had unwittingly made my first dirty joke. It was explained that I had to ask about *chicken's* eggs, otherwise I would be understood as asking how the male passengers' genitals were holding up.

After a while longer, we pulled up by a rough shed and drank coffee while the driver unloaded coconuts. There was a lengthy discussion about whether or not the correct coconuts were being removed. 'See,' said the owner, 'I have written my name on them in biro.' I thought of the cave in Londa, just outside town, where the skulls of the dead have been identified by writing their names on them in ballpoint. The trade in coconuts was a strange one. Some would ship them up the mountain, others ship them down. Possibly the same coconuts were going up and down in a weird antique-dealer's economy.

We sat on a rough wooden bench, looking on. Johannis seemed troubled. 'The driver,' he explained, 'is trying to make Bambang ill. But, you see, Bambang goes on with his journey even though he suffers. Bambang is foolish but not a coward. It is the driver who is stupid.'

Thoughts about the injustice of the world were interrupted by a large, smouldering log that flew low over our heads, followed by a demented cackling.

A stick-like old woman lurched into view, toothless and dreadlocked. She wore a torn, filthy frock that had once been decorated with a heavy floral pattern. A thick layer of filth caked her face and arms and in her hand she waved another log menacingly. Johannis and I looked at each other. 'Mad?' I asked. 'Mad, indeed,' he replied. In wordless agreement we took to our heels and from inside the hut regarded her through the wire-covered window.

She stood outside and sang a song in Japanese, applauded by the passengers. Then came a ditty apparently about American foreign policy during the Sukarno era. I felt I was being given a lesson in political history. Hard on the heels of this followed a song concerning the sexual *mores* of present-day Indonesian leaders that brought either giggles or growls of protest from the men and led the women to cover their noses in outraged modesty. As for myself, it showed the holes in my vocabulary.

The driver shooed her away and she contented herself with writing rude words in the dust on the sides of the vehicle and begging for small coins that were nervously yielded up.

The driver leant back and whispered in the tones of one delivering a great secret, 'She is a schoolteacher driven mad by her learning.' He paused. 'Are you a schoolteacher?' I thought of Godfrey Butterfield MA. He would have approved.

'Something like that.'

We set off again through a drizzle that hissed in the trees. Torajaland is one of those rare places where banana-trees flourish next to mountain pines. The road climbed again into the cloud. It felt intensely cold. Abruptly we came to a halt on a mournful plateau covered with scrubby grass. A goat, munching on it, regarded us with detachment. The engine was cut and the world was silent apart from the sound of running water and the scrunching of the goat. A young man climbed out and moved towards a distant house – not a noble structure of carved wood but a shack of haphazard appearance. Women came out and stood crying in desperate wailings that left them gasping for breath. Suddenly, the young man began to sob, his head falling on his chest and big, wet tears streaming down his cheeks. Other men climbed out and hugged each other, crying in the mist. 'He cries because his friend is dead,' explained the driver. It seemed that a ferry had capsized between Malaysia and Sumatra. Many of the sailors had been Torajan, for the area is such a tough place to make a living that it is one of the few landlocked mountain regions to produce seamen in large numbers. Many had been drowned. The driver and Bambang got out too and clung wetly together with the others in the rain. Embarrassed, I descended and stood to one side, not wishing to intrude on their grief, staring out over the sodden landscape as if engrossed in contemplation of the goat. An arm reached out, groped blindly at my shoulder and, seizing me by the elbow, pulled me into their world of fellow-feeling. I began to cry too.

I have no idea how long we stood sobbing in the rain. It may have been for ten minutes, possibly much longer. When we returned to the bus, we were all somehow shriven and chastened, more like brothers are supposed to be but never quite are. The driver now avoided the potholes and blew no more cigarette smoke in Bambang's eyes. The conversation turned to the harsh life of the seafarer, how he returns from a long voyage and is stripped of his earnings by rapacious relatives. Slowly, we began to laugh again.

Emerging on the summit of a hill, we saw the town of Pangala' stretched out below us. It would take another half-hour of twisting and turning down the slope before we would reach it. It was another wooden shanty town, awash with schoolchildren. 'When I came down the mountain to go to school here,' said Johannis, 'I used to have to carry a sack of rice twelve kilometres so I would have enough to eat. I was strong then. After so many years in town, I am weak.'

We disembarked into another coffee shop as yet another rain squall swept down upon us. Once again people came from the kitchen to look at this strange man – strange not because I was white but because I had asked for coffee without sugar. On the wall was a condom displayed in a glass case like a trophy – part of the family-planning campaign. We learnt, however, that we were in luck. There was a cement truck going up the road to Johannis's village, carrying material for the new middle school. We would be able to buy a lift.

Bambang wandered away but many of the other passengers transferred to the truck – including the coconuts. Ropes had been strung the length of the back and we insinuated ourselves into them or draped ourselves over them after the fashion of a flophouse.

'The road is a little difficult,' confessed Johannis. Indeed a different fare was charged for going up the mountain and for coming back down. It had clearly not been repaired for years and deep pools lowered expectantly at the most inconvenient places. The principal difficulty lay in the tyres of the truck, which were so completely bald that they could grip nothing at all. Where a normal truck would have sailed through mud, ours stopped and slithered helplessly. Where a normal truck would have chugged up inclines, ours simply churned great holes in the road to the smell of burning rubber.

Whenever we became bogged down, the procedure was the same. At first, we would sit tight and pretend not to notice the difficulty. *'Turun! Dorong!'* would shout the driver. 'Get down and push!' We would clamber down and mill around. Some would watch while others pushed. Then, when almost enough were pushing to get us out, the rest would join in – at which point half the original pushers would stop. Getting a truck out of mud is something everyone has a theory about.

'Planks!' said one man firmly. 'What we need is planks.'

'But don't you think if the tyres were …?'

'No. Planks.'

Some believed firmly that the thing to do was to shovel mud from in front of the truck and throw it behind the rear wheels. Most of it ended up being sprayed over the pushers. Some would push grass and leaves under the wheels, whence they would be studiously removed by those of a different conviction. Yet others set their faith in rocks. Nothing but rocks would do and they dug them from the road and pushed them under the spinning tyres with naked feet at horrendous risk. One old man dismantled the ropes with painful care and began to pull from the front in a lone, heroic gesture. Johannis sat down and smoked a cigarette while joking with the girls. When it seemed that all hope was past, a man sauntered by with a huge buffalo led by a tiny boy. The little boy calmly hitched it to the front of the truck and it pulled us out with contemptuous ease. A voice came from behind. 'It would have been easier with planks.'

'I thought Torajans didn't use buffaloes for physical labour,' I said to Johannis.

'That,' he declared, 'is a slave buffalo. Look at the colour.'

Anthropologists are raised on books about the Nuer, a Sudanese people who seem obsessed with cattle and their beauty. They have developed a rich vocabulary of colour and pattern to describe their beasts. This was my first lesson in a similar Torajan obsession, a seemingly endless series of terms to describe buffalo size and colour and pattern and horn-shape. It would later be the same when I worked with carvers – an infinite string of discriminations between patterns that I would have classed as the same.

Johannis, tiring of abstract lexicography, embarked on a much more relevant topic. Should the driver not give us a reduction for the great distance we had actually walked while putatively riding in his truck? Should *he* not, indeed, be paying *us* since it was only thanks to our labour as pushers that he was able to deliver his cement at all? The driver, to give him credit, saw the force of Johannis's argument. So strongly, indeed, did he appreciate it as a threat to his continued livelihood that I soon found myself ejected from the truck and condemned to walk into the village along with Johannis. 'That man,' declared Johannis, 'is an enemy of my family. He is of slave descent.'

'I thought it was only in the southern kingdoms that they had all those social classes, gold class, bronze class, iron class and so on.'

'Maybe,' said Johannis huffily, 'but we know a slave for a slave even if we're not supposed to use the word any more.'

Be that as it might, this was the first time I had ever made enemies before even arriving in a field-work location. I began to wonder if Johannis was not too clever by half to be a field assistant – for I suddenly realized that this was what he had become.

Johannis's house was a modern structure, based on the Buginese bungalows of the coast. Built on stilts to mitigate the torrid heat of those areas, it was clear that it would prove bitterly cold at night. We paused to be barked at by a dog, remove our shoes and climb a ladder to the front door, where I cracked my head on the lintel to the considerable pleasure of onlookers. For a Westerner, life in Indonesia is a series of blows to the head. The whole country is built on the assumption that you are not more that five foot six tall. The only time I really hated Indonesians was after a particularly hard crack on the head. As the mist of pain cleared, you would open your eyes to see a group of ecstatically happy brown faces laughing at you. Someone would usually explain that you had hit your head because you were too tall.

Johannis's mother had clearly been a beautiful woman in her youth, with delicate features and a natural grace that shone through the torn clothes and careworn face. It was immediately obvious that she was also a deeply pious woman. The house was adorned with an odd mixture of religious symbols. On one wall were the obligatory photographs of the President and his deputy, flanked by the Space Shuttle and the Last Supper – a version clearly after Leonardo but with all the disciples endowed with huge staring blue eyes, like lunatics. Then came a vaguely biblical image involving sheep and children. Last year's calendar showed

Muslim pin-ups of ladies swathed in loose folds of cloth against a background of mosques and sacred texts. This year's offered semi-naked Chinese whose attractions were largely blanked out by a censoriously placed mirror.

Only later did anyone bother to introduce Johannis's father, a worn, shrivelled man who wore the embittered look of one used to being publicly discounted as of no significance. Johannis and his mother embarked on a long account of his doings, his sins of omission and commission. It seemed that he drank, idled, did not go to church. We exchanged glances of mute sympathy.

From the kitchen came clattering noises and puffs of wood-smoke. Various hunched relatives scuttled in and out in the crouched posture of respect before a guest. We were served sickly-sweet coffee in glasses, while the mother switched to Indonesian to detail her many woes – her poverty, her bad leg, her wastrel husband, her feckless sons, the shortage of onions in the village. Torajans who have not been school-taught find it difficult to pronounce the 'ch' sound and some of the consonantal clusters of Indonesian, so that *kecil,* 'small', comes out *ketil,* and *pergi,* 'go', comes out *piggi.* It gives their speech a strange, Shirley Temple-like quality of lisping coyness. She concluded, 'We are old. We have no hope. The boys have all left to go to the city. We pray for a good death, if God opens the way.' It was a depressing sort of welcome and Johannis was already turning grumpy in the classic way of an ambitious youth ashamed of his parents.

Various other people drifted in – a cousin, a half-brother. The men were fed a meal of rice and chilli and – absurdly – we were required to rest on mattresses that were unfurled in the middle of the room while the female activities of the house raged about us.

Gradually, it became clear that the day was being classed as over, despite the fact that it was barely late afternoon. At nightfall, a glaring-eyed neighbour came to light the oil-lamp – a complex, pressurized affair that no one in the house could master. He, too, joined us in the bed and more and more blankets were heaped over us against the penetrating chill. A strange mould made them glow in the dark. Finally, the mat was taken off the floor and added as well. It was with some pride that I revealed my hot-water bottle. You have to be a real Old Hand to take one of those to the tropics. It was an instant success. Feet probed inexpertly for it.

Even Johannis was impressed. 'I expect when you go home you will leave this behind.'

Night fell and we all lay awake telling stories, bright-eyed and excited like little boys on a camping trip. Someone told of a Buginese magician he had seen in Ujung Pandang. 'He set up a spear and put a melon on top. It fell down. It was split. Then he took this little boy, five or six he must have been, and balanced him on the spear on his navel and spun him round. We all covered our faces expecting blood. But he was unhurt.'

'Wah!'

'That is nothing,' said Johannis. 'I know these Chinese girls, two sisters. You write anything on a piece of paper, tear it up, put it in a matchbox. They hold it under their armpits like this (he squashed his arms against his body) and they can tell you what you wrote.'

'Wah!'

Their eyes turned in silent interrogation to me. Here was an exotic foreigner, one who had seen the wonders of the world. Who knew what I would come up with?

'Once,' I said, 'I met a man in Africa who could control the rain.'

'Yawn! Yes we have that too.' They sounded bored.

'I once lived with people who cut off human heads and collected them.'

'Oh, we used to do that. What of it?'

'Once I went hunting lions with only a spear.'

'I expect it's the same as we do with the dwarf buffalo that lives in the forest except buffalo would be even more dangerous.'

They were already turning on their sides to sleep. It was time for the big one. I reached in my back pocket and drew out a plastic credit card.

'This', I said, 'is like money.' They sat up and examined it in the flickering light, sliding the rays over the holographic image embedded in it. It was solemnly passed from one to another.

'In my country, in the towns, there are machines in the walls. You can put these in and type a number and the machine will give you money.'

'Wah! Wah! Wah!'

They carefully passed it back and we all settled to sleep. I dreamt of spears and Chinese wizards. I don't know what they dreamt of.

An anthropologist is probably the worst of guests imaginable. I would not have one in the house. He comes unrequested, settles in uninvited and plagues his hosts with foolish questions to the point of distraction. Initially he will have little idea what it is that he is looking for. How, after all, do you capture the essence of an alien way of life? Anthropologists do not even agree among themselves what sort of quarry they are hunting – whether it is to be found in people's heads, in the concrete facts of external reality, in both or in neither. Others would view most of anthropological 'knowledge' as a fiction created somewhere between the observer and the observed and dependent on the unequal relations of power between the two. The almost inevitable response is to get on with it and analyse precisely what it was you did later.

In my own case, it was easy to decide where to start. Johannis announced that we were to set off that very morning to a *ma'nene'* festival. We should be accompanied by his grandfather on the walk there some five or six kilometres away. Indeed, there in the kitchen sat a sedate old gentleman chewing on a lump of boiled manioc, carrying a spear with its blade sheathed. He laughed companionably at the mere sight of me and offered a chew on the manioc that he then slid into his pocket to finish later.

The whole village seemed to be in motion. Children leaned out of the houses to stare. They could not get their tongues around *Belanda*, 'Dutchman', so they called out *Bandala*, 'box', instead. From the houses issued a stream of people most of whom were wearing black, the colour of death. The two classes of Torajan festivals were segregated here too, those of the west and 'descending smoke' – the festivals of death – and those of the east and 'rising smoke' – the festivals of life. Torajan ritual seems totally lopsided, to emphasize death rather than life. This, however, may well be due to the influence of missionaries who have suppressed the relatively licentious rites of fertility, leaving those of death as incongruous as a beached whale. Different forms of Christianity have reached different compromises with the old way. Some churches insist that their devotees must absent themselves from certain parts of the death festivals and not eat buffalo of sacrifice. Others require the faithful to offer buffalo to the church. Some concentrate on the grave images, a Christian must not have one and that is that. Others permit an image as long as it is regarded as a mere memorial.

All around, greetings were being exchanged and there was a good deal of giggling. Johannis's grandfather kept himself aloof, his face marked with the *gravitas* of a butler at an orgy. 'I do not speak much Indonesian,' he explained, 'but I want you to know that in this village I am the old religion. These people are now Christian but still they have to heed what I say. I have declared *ma'nene*'. Now there can be no cultivation of the fields or building of houses until I end it. Even Christians keep to that.'

I turned to Johannis. 'You are Christian too?'

'Yes, I am a Protestant like yourself but for us young people it is less important. We have ...' he groped for a word, '... wider thought than the people of Nenek's generation.'

Nenek snorted. 'When I was young, I was the same. When I wanted to start learning the religion, the old poetry, they all begged me not to. They said I would always be poor. They were right but there are more important things. He too will learn. He is not a stupid boy.'

On a hilltop stood a church, whitewashed with a spire after the Tyrolean fashion. Behind it stretched row after row of purple brooding hills with no sign of human habitation. Through a gap in the clouds, an Old Testament sky poured light down upon the roof. It looked like the loneliest church in the world. As we walked along, a stream of observations and interpretations poured from the old man with the ease of a sports commentator – history, myths, personal recollections. Many cultures have licensed pundits, their own indigenous anthropologists. They occasionally loom large in the literature of the subject, their names known to generations of students. I had never met one before but Nenek was clearly one of these. I had an assistant. My specialist informant had now appeared. Even though I was only here for a derisorily short time, it was impossible not to start work. With something akin to a groan, I pulled out a notebook and started writing it all down.

A considerable crowd had gathered at the base of a sheer cliff whose face was pocked with square openings. These were the tombs in which the bones of the dead were stored. Unlike other parts of Torajaland, there were no wooden figures, here to represent the dead, each tomb being simply sealed with a wooden panel carved with a buffalo head. In the past, Johannis maintained, there had been such images but now they had all disappeared. At the present festival, the bones of the newly dead were wrapped in fresh cloths and put back in the tombs. A man had been down to the city to buy the cloths specially. Surprisingly, they were of the most garish colours and livid with prints of Mickey Mouse and Donald Duck.

I had hoped to slide in undetected, to creep quietly into a corner and assume the voyeuristic pose of the ethnographer. It was not to be. Nenek was a performer. This was his big event and he was going to make the most of it. We approached through dense undergrowth, invisible to the crowd. Slipping behind a rock just outside the circle of participants, Nenek produced a series of rustlings and gruntings, calling out testily to Johannis to help him. In a few minutes, he emerged transformed, dressed in a red striped outfit with short trousers and sleeves. I remembered one of the exercises from my Indonesian primer. 'The caterpillar has changed to become a butterfly.' Nenek beamed and wrestled with the fastening of his necklace, a weighty affair that looked like a string of gold-plated toilet rolls. On top, Johannis draped a chain of boar-tusks that contrived to poke Nenek in the ears. The old man adjusted gold bracelets in the form of snakes writhing up his arms and looked round distractedly for his spear.

Seizing me by the arm as just another prop, he leaped out into the stunned circle of villagers and launched into a lengthy speech, poking me from time to time with the spear to illustrate a point. Johannis rested one hand reassuringly on my shoulder and seemed unsure whether to be proud or ashamed of his aged relative.

'He is explaining who you are, that you are a famous Dutch tourist, that you are here to honour us and the old ways.' From time to time, his voice would rise and settle into a rhythm that, even to an outsider, was the mark of poetry. 'That's *to minaa* talk,' whispered Johannis, 'the language of the old way. I can't translate it but – wah, it's beautiful!'

Finally it was over and Nenek settled on a rock in the centre of the open ground, pointing and rebuking, dominating the efforts of others, grumpily cradling his spear in his arms.

Access to the tombs involves climbing notched bamboo poles some sixty or seventy feet above the ground while manhandling the corpse into the narrow tomb-opening. Several of the sailors from the bus seemed to be in charge of this and they hailed me like an old friend. Would I like to climb up? No? Then perhaps I would like to eat. They themselves, as Christians, were not really supposed to eat a buffalo that had been sacrificed at the tombs, but …

We settled to a meal in the shade of a large tree. 'No rice,' they explained, 'because of death. We eat only manioc – and buffalo.' The buffalo was tough and sinewy with a thick integument of fat and skin. Each section looked like a boiled slug. The sun was high and uncomfortably hot. A pleasant smell of wood-smoke, buffalo fat and warm humanity hung over the tombs, with the drowsy hum of flies feasting on the blood. Johannis had been deputed to haul a body ready to be replaced in the tomb and stood in the sun, grinning and brushing the heat out of his thick black hair.

Nenek began shouting again and a head appeared in the tomb-mouth and let down a rope to be tied to the corpse. The whole occasion was one of somewhat unseemly enjoyment. The rope was slung about the package of cloth and bones to the accompaniment of a great deal of knockabout humour. As it was hauled into the air, Johannis leapt astride it like a bronco buster and emitted a series of whoops that the other young men took up until Nenek shook with rage and the effort of remonstration.

A circle of men formed up beneath and began the slow death-chant, linking hands in an impassive anti-clockwise rotation. Children were called to join in, fathers and brothers gently guiding their steps into the ancient rhythms. At a signal from Nenek, women infiltrated the circle, men and women calling back and forth to each other in song – a song of death but one in which the ladies were not slow to show their fine profiles and flash perfect teeth. Nenek nodded in approval, his hand marking the pulses of the haunting melody. It hardly looked like a society split by religious change.

One of the sailors suggested that it would be polite to meet the organizer of the festival. I was led away to a group standing around a cauldron of steaming water.

'This is the head,' he said, tapping one man on the shoulder. He turned round. It was Hitler.

'Ah,' said Hitler, 'I already know this gentleman.'

I rapidly began to think of excuses and explanations but there was, it seemed, no need. Indeed, he began to apologize to me.

'There has been a difficulty regarding that object,' he whispered. 'I no longer have it. It was confiscated by the police. But I hope shortly to have another and I will contact you again.'

I assured him I would await his visit with bated breath and returned to my seat, sweating profusely.

One rather stout lady seemed worthy of special note for, despite the great heat, she was wearing a thick fur coat and waving at me as at an old friend.

'Who is that?' I asked the sailors. They giggled.

'That is "Dutch Auntie". She lives in Leiden and has come all the way back for this festival. She wears her coat of dog-fur to show how rich she has become in your country.'

Noting that we were talking about her, she broke away and came to join us, greeting me in Dutch.

'Sorry,' I replied in Indonesian, 'I'm not really Dutch but English.'

'Never mind!' she replied. 'You're a Westerner like me. I live there now you know. Look how pale I have become. I suffer so when I come to Toraja – the heat, the dirt. In Holland we go everywhere by taxi.'

Johannis appeared behind her, ill disposed to listen to her pretensions. 'Ah. I remember you. You used to run a noodle stall near the market.' He cleared his throat and spat.

If looks could kill. Johannis would have dropped on the spot. Dutch Auntie gathered her fur coat about her sweat-bedewed shoulders and stalked off. This was a foolhardy act since she was wearing high heels unsuited to loose rock and she insisted on covering her departure by offering a sickly smile and a wave of the hand over one shoulder. One moment she was there, a focus of pathetic affectation that somehow made *me* feel ashamed. The next she had gone – plunging over the ledge on to the dancers below. Fortunately no one was hurt. She was later to be seen sitting under a tree while a child fanned her with a banana leaf, all the while wearing her fur coat and asking the names of things, since, as she constantly explained, she spoke so much Dutch she had forgotten almost all Torajan.

In the course of the day, a considerable number of bodies were wrapped and replaced in their respective tombs. On the following day, Nenek would kill a chicken and declare the end of the festival. Then people could go back to growing crops and building houses – the activities associated with life. It was now almost dark and time to head back to the village.

Dutch Auntie collected together her kin and set off in one direction. I, Nenek, Johannis and a group of neighbours set off in another. A young man, leading his son by the hand, invited me in excellent, almost courtly, Indonesian to visit his house near by. It was a fine old building, richly carved and decorated in the local style.

'This,' he said with evident pride, 'is my house. From my

ancestors for generations. Those are my fields. My grandfather worked them when I was a boy. Now I work them in turn.'

Nenek was fretful. He wanted to get back to his end of the village before dark but the man who introduced himself as Andareus was gently persistent in his hospitality.

Inside, the traditional house had, like all others I had visited, reached its own compromises with the modern world. A large ghetto-blaster stood threateningly in one corner next to a hideous sideboard carved with traditional Torajan patterns but coloured with gloss paint. Yet this was still an ancient house where ancient patterns of generosity were maintained. Andareus pointed out of the window. 'My mother keeps on at me to put in a modern bathroom and fill in the bottom of the house with cement but I tell her to bathe in the stream is better and that we must respect an old house. Otherwise it is like an old woman in the clothes of a bar-girl.'

We drank coffee and ate the special cakes of palm-sugar that are a Torajan token of hospitality. Both father and son wore black sarongs, not the shorts that are now almost ubiquitous. It was good to meet a man who seemed to have resisted much of the worst of the modern world, a man of clear intelligence and charm who seemed content to stay in this remote village and cultivate his garden. But such categories were mine rather than his.

'Where did you learn such splendid Indonesian?' I asked. 'Are you a teacher?'

He grinned and switched casually to idiomatic American. 'I guess I learnt most at Massachusetts Institute of Technology,' he confided, 'when I did my master's in satellite communications. Before I could learn English, I had to do intensive courses in my own national language.' He grinned and poked his son affectionately. 'This one speaks English and Indonesian as his first languages but when we come here he can't talk to his grandmother. He gets real bored. Where I work in Kalimantan we have a swimming pool and a video. He misses that. We only came back for the festival – to rewrap my father's body. He thinks it's a lot of bother over a stiff.'

My disappointment must have been evident. Westerners have an inherent tendency to use the rest of the world to think about their own problems. Andareus was no 'noble savage' pointing out the inadequacies of our own world. He was rather more of a modern man than I was – fluent with the jargon of computer and electronics. His values were probably much the same as mine. His attachment to the traditional world was as much an outsider's as my own was. It was seen from the comfort of an air-conditioned modern bungalow in Kalimantan, possibly just a kind of romanticism. He rubbed salt into my wounds by his relentless self-awareness.

'You see, I only learned to value the old way by going abroad. If I had sat in my village I would have thought of America as the Kingdom of Heaven. So I come back for the festivals. For years we have been leaving the mountains to make a living but we always come back to spend the money here in festivals. This one,' he gestured towards his son, 'is different. He knows little of the old way. He grew up abroad. He's not a Torajan. He's modern Indonesia.'

Modern Indonesia contemplated us with equanimity, scratching at a mosquito bite.

We set off through the lowering gloom towards the village. Fine dust lay soft under our feet like sand on a tropical beach. Nenek strode away at a pace Johannis and I found hard to match. At a corner in the road that overlooked a dramatic gorge stood a man wrapped in a blue blanket, only shifting over five feet in height but sporting a magnificent lush moustache. He grinned delightedly and shook me by the hand. Not quite knowing how to show friendliness, I admired the buffalo he was guarding, on the principle that if you make friends with a man's dog, you make friends with him.

'This,' he declared, 'is how I spend my time making arrangements for my buffalo.'

'Do you have many buffalo?'

'Just one.'

'How is it possible to spend all day making arrangements for just one buffalo?'

Nenek barked his amusement and, in a gesture I was to come to know well, pointed a closed hand at me (the polite way of pointing at someone), helpless with laughter.

'The number has nothing to do with it. It is like a young man who has much hair. He just rubs his hand through it, and it looks good. As he gets older, he has less hair, so it takes him longer and longer to arrange it. So it is with buffalo.'

The buffalo-man laughed too. In fact, of course, both he and Nenek, like most Torajans, had indecently prolific hair.

'If I had more buffalo,' said the man, 'I would be a lord cat.'

'What's a lord cat?'

'It's a special sort of cat that sits at home and never leaves the house. It never touches the ground. It would be afraid.'

'What does it look like?'

'It looks like other cats except that it never leaves the house – unless the owner carries it to the rice-barn to kill mice.'

We talked more about the creature until we arrived at the bridge. Like many Torajan bridges it had a roof and seats were built into it. Bridges make ideal places to gossip on rainy days. From the buffalo-man I learned that lord cats are expected to guard heirlooms that are stored in the rafters of noble houses and in the barns opposite them. They should only mate with other lord cats brought by their owners to the house for that purpose. Once again, the Torajans were talking about their own class system through animals. The cats, with their heirlooms and restricted mating patterns, were modelled on, and models for, noble families.

We parted to trudge to our separate houses but the rain managed to catch us in that relatively short space. We arrived back soaked and shivering. It seemed the right moment to break out a bottle of King Adam whisky, secreted in my baggage. The name 'whisky' is a term of misapplied courtesy or extreme irony. The contents are rice-spirit coloured with caramel. Nenek looked at it doubtfully.

'It is good when you are cold like this,' I explained, 'like medicine.'

'Medicine?' He homed in on the word. Soon he was sipping it appreciatively, but from a teaspoon summoned from the kitchen. Johannis's father entered coughing, cast a hopeful glance at the bottle and was about to accept some until his wife appeared and looked righteously at him from the door. Crestfallen, he returned the glass to the table.

'I do not drink spirits,' he announced uncertainly.

'This,' said Nenek, 'is making me strong. Come to my house tomorrow so we can talk. Johannis will bring you.'

'What time?'

He looked at me pityingly. 'I have no watch. Just come.'

He gathered up his props and leaned over the balcony to propel mucus with neat pressure from one nostril. Pausing at the door to shuffle on plastic sandals, he turned round and grinned wickedly.

'That medicine,' he said in courtly fashion, 'could I take the rest of it with me? It really seems to be doing me good.' He shuffled off into the dusk.

It was the appropriate moment to raise a delicate matter.

'Where,' I asked, 'is the place to "cast water"?' Johannis gestured vaguely.

'We use those banana trees down there for small water. For large water it's a bit difficult here. You have to go and stand in one of the streams.'

'Where do you wash?'

'There is a place near the bridge. It is too cold to wash.'

'Would you show me where it is?'

He grumbled good-naturedly but finally sighed. 'I will come with you. You will need to wear a sarong. I have stolen little packets of soap from the hotel.'

A Torajan bathroom is a wonderful thing. It is a simple rock enclosure into which fresh mountain water gushes through a bamboo pipe. Modesty is preserved by fixing a stick across the opening and draping a sarong over it. This system works well for those about five feet tall. For anyone over that height, all is revealed. Since, however, it was dark that would not be a problem. Johannis pressed a bar of soap into my hand. We took turns to stand under the thunderous waterfall. He was right. It *was* too cold but very refreshing. We both seemed to be having a similar problem with the soap, however. It doggedly refused to lather. The water must be very hard. Only when we returned to the house and the light of the paraffin lamp did the reason become clear. It was not soap that he had stolen but little bars of chocolate. We had smeared them all over ourselves.

Morning comes to an Indonesian village with a dramatic intensity that is almost comical. It begins with the cockerels, strutting around arrogantly, issuing tedious challenges to the world and scrabbling with their claws on corrugated iron roofs. Dogs join in, then donkeys, horses, cats, pigeons and children, screaming and trumpeting a fierce, all-encompassing din that heaves you out of bed. Then comes rice-pounding, the relentless thud of pestle on mortar that makes the whole house shake till you feel queasy. The final touch is added by the inevitable cassette-player that belts out the same, insistent six pop-songs over and over again while anyone not pounding rice gives voice to gargles of thick phlegm and leisurely nose-clearing.

Then comes a long stage of people staggering about in various degrees of physical distress, groping for the first, desperate cigarette, throwing cold water over themselves with the gasps of drowning men and great expectorations, or roaming the house with baffled expressions on their faces, constantly readjusting sarongs and sucking air through their teeth as they hug themselves and shiver.

All over the village, people are crouching miserably in corners discussing the cold. They huddle round the fire, whose embers have been poked into life to the annoyance of the cat who invariably sleeps there. The misery knows no end until the sun finally penetrates the chill and brings back life to the village. Like the English summer, the morning cold seems to constantly amaze everyone and no attempt is ever made to prepare against it. My Mamasa blanket was much admired, though no one in the village had bothered to acquire one for himself and no one wove there any more. In the mornings there was often much talk of a Dutch house that had once stood in the village and boasted a stove. When it was really cold, people would take refuge there. But, alas, a landslide had destroyed it.

After a meal of warmed-up leftovers and sweet coffee, we set off. By now the sun was high and Johannis was sure we would find Nenek up to his thighs in mud, ploughing his rice-field. We did a little tourism, climbing up the road of exploded cobbles that led to the forest and the high peaks. Johannis pointed out a slab of rock that rose vertically out of the valley floor.

'That,' he explained, 'is the fort of Pong Tiku.' I knew of him as the Torajan leader who had fought the Dutch when they moved into the area in 1906. After a long siege, he was defeated.

'What happened to him?'

'The Dutch took him to Rantepao and shot him.' A look of fury crossed his face. 'Nowadays he is a hero, but Baruppu' people fought him. He burnt the village and everyone fled to Makki to seek magic. Just as we were about to return and destroy him, the Dutch came. That is why there are no really old houses here.'

We moved on through elegant stands of bamboo that insisted on framing vistas of incredible beauty. The hills were punctuated with gushing streams, many of which could be crossed only via bridges of slippery green bamboo poles. Johannis took great joy in assisting me across like an old man.

We came to another hamlet, standing on the top of a hill. Until now I had been struck by the tidiness and order of Torajan villages. They even planted flowers and shared that most English of notions, the lawn. This one was different. It was a mess. Nowhere else had I seen pigs allowed to wander freely and forage as they pleased. They had churned up the space between the houses into a quagmire. The people all looked slightly sticky and disreputable. Children ran everywhere mewling and holding handfuls of glutinous mess to their mouths. All had snot-trails under their noses. It looked as if someone had been collecting evidence to disprove the notion that Man had been made in the image of God. Suddenly, there emerged from one of the houses a man of contrasting kemptness. For a second, I thought it was Bambang, the architect, but it was another similar. He wore a spotless white shirt and trousers, polished shoes and a large gold watch. His hair was elegantly coiffed and parted as with a ruler. With elegant syntax, he invited us in. A corpse lay in the corner, wrapped for some future interment. Occasionally someone would get up and hit a gong.

The kempt man launched into a violent denunciation of the villagers. He had, he assured me, written to the President about their backwardness, but strangely received no reply. But then, the President was a busy man. He had prayed to God that they all be struck down but God was clearly busy too. Still, one or two had been hit. He continued in a similar vein with much head-shaking and suddenly stood and delivered an impromptu sermon in a high-pitched scream. It was hard to know what religion he drew on, since Torajan Christians refer to God as Allah too. But it was clearly a God of the sword and he was impressively articulate.

The other villagers sat around giggling and whispering. Johannis watched me smugly. Then, the penny dropped.

'Is this man perhaps a schoolteacher?' I hissed. They all grinned and nodded. 'Driven mad by his learning?' They grinned and nodded again. The madman continued preaching. He was now talking about lightning.

'He is not dangerous,' explained Johannis, 'and his family look after him. But he is very boring.'

"Yes, I can see that.'

'Life has become much easier since they bought him the bicycle.'

'The bicycle?'

'Yes, now instead of preaching to them, he can cycle down to the market and preach to everyone.'

We continued on our way, climbing up towards the forest. After a while we came to a small hamlet of very beautiful traditional houses, the tallest I had seen. They were quite new and exhibited some unusual features. In one of the windows, traditionally placed high up in the gables, had been covered by two nude pin-ups in accordance with modern taste. The carving was deeper and the motifs were bigger than those I had seen down in the valley. At the far end was a ramshackle structure that might easily be converted to a warm family home but was manifestly permanently in course of arrangement. The veranda that had been planned for the front was still in a rudimentary stage, with unfastened planks simply laid across the beams so that they could flip up in the face of the incautious visitor. The wooden handrail to the access stairs was broken and tied with string. The roof was an incongruous mixture of wooden slats and corrugated iron that was a mere temporary expedient. The beams were festooned with bags and woodworking tools. It was the house of a builder, a man far too busy sorting out other people's houses ever to get round to his own. Here sat Nenek, carving a large beam. He was not just a priest of the old religion, he was a woodcarver too.

I motioned to Johannis to stop and we paused to watch. Nenek was totally absorbed in his work. On his nose was perched a pair of glasses as ramshackle as his house. The hands that had been frail and dry as sticks were now firm as he guided the knife in smooth, delicate curves. A curiosity of Nenek's hands, the long curvature of the thumbs, was now revealed as the result of many years' pressure from the carving knife. His hands glided over the black surface of the beam with the elegance of an ice-skater, curls of wood snaking out between his fingers as the delicate spirals and loops of the geometric pattern leapt out from the background. It was one of the most therapeutic moments I have ever known, a sense of peace reigned over the hamlet, a feeling of smooth serenity. Nenek leaned forward and spat and I had a sudden horrified realization that his spittle was bright red. Was he seriously ill, a dying tubercular artist in these damp hills? Then I saw the jaws champing, the areca-nut lying beside the beam. He was chewing the bitter nut with lime after the fashion of many old Torajans whose teeth are turned mahogany by the red juice.

It seemed a shame that this was happening in total isolation. I felt the urge to share the moment with someone, to fix the pleasure. Johannis yawned hugely. But why *shouldn't* other people see this? It would make a wonderful exhibition. I could take Nenek to London so he could build a carved house or a rice-barn. The exhibition would not be just the finished object but the whole process of its construction. The moment that the thought was complete, I rejected it. Just imagine the problems with visas, wood, funding. Perhaps Nenek would get ill. Perhaps it was an immoral action, an urge to convert people into performing animals. Anyway, it could never be done. Nenek looked up, saw us and cackled.

We spent the rest of the day watching him work. He talked of the patterns, their names and meanings, of the stories relating to house-building. He had risen early that day to end the period of *ma'nene'* so that creative activities could be resumed. It was good to have a knife back in his hands. But, alas, tomorrow he would have to stop again since the body in the mad schoolteacher's village was to be finally dealt with. The dead man was of the old religion, so Nenek would be in charge.

As we were about to leave the hamlet, a man beckoned Johannis over and they had a long whispered conversation. Finally, he turned to me and grinned. *'Makan angin?'* he inquired – 'Eating the wind?' an idiom that means to go for a walk without any fixed purpose. 'Yes,' I agreed with the vacuous good humour required of the field-worker, *'Makan angin.'*

Johannis laughed. 'No,' he said. 'Not *angin*-wind, *anjing*-dog. We are lucky. A dog has caught rabies in the village and been killed so we can eat it. You will not be cold tonight. Dog is very hot!'

The next day's ceremony was a somewhat rustic and rough-hewn version of the one I had seen in the valley. Although Nenek was in overall command and once more very much on his dignity, most of the actual work was done by a man in a sailor's cap. For once, there was a surplus of meat piled up in the path – dead pigs and buffalo. An auction began, pieces being sold off at what seemed like rather high prices. There were no tourists here. I was glad not to fall into that unflattering category. I was here as a guest, not because they wanted anything from me.

'Thank you again for that medicine you gave me,' said Nenek. Medicine? Ah yes, the whisky.

'But it is not good to drink medicine without meat. Perhaps you would like to buy me that piece of pig they are selling.'

I decided to try a little sarcasm.

'I hear there is dog for sale. Perhaps you would prefer that.'

'No. Dog makes you very strong with women. I am old. It would not be seemly.' I decided to try to change the subject.

'How old are you, Nenek?'

'Over a hundred.'

'He's seventy,' said Johannis. They glared at each other.

'In those days, we did not count,' resumed Nenek. 'I was born in the year there were many mice. An old man needs to eat pig.'

I sighed and bought him the pig.

The idea of the exhibition would not go away. But how could I get a mountain man to grasp such an alien concept? It would have to be handled carefully. I did not want to alarm Nenek by suddenly coming out with it.

'Nenek, suppose I wanted to build a carved rice-barn in London. Could it be done?'

'Of course. I'll come and do it if you like. Shall we leave today? I'll need three helpers, Johannis, Tanduk over there and a special man if you want a bamboo roof. I can give you a list of all the pieces of wood we'll need. We won't argue about the price. One really good buffalo is the standard rate for me. You'll have to give something to the others though. We'll need some coolies in England too.'

'Coolies?'

'Yes, to help with the lifting.'

'Aren't you worried about going to a strange country?'

'Why should I be? Carvers are used to working away from their village when there's a job to be done. Anyway,' he squeezed my hand, 'I know you will look after us and protect us if there are enemies.'

'It will take a lot of time to plan, Nenek. I cannot promise you. I shall have to persuade the English and then the Indonesians to let us do it. It will be *very* difficult.'

'Is there wood in England?'

'It's not the right wood. We would have to bring everything from here.'

'That is no problem. We can choose the wood. Is there areca-nut to eat in England?'

'There is no areca-nut.'

'*That* might be a problem. Never mind. You and I will do it together. When they wanted a Torajan house for the exhibition in Jakarta, they took a man from Kesu. He has never stopped boasting about it. *This* will stop him.' He stared into the distance with a visionary gleam in his eye. For some reason, I could only think of the problem of sending a bill to the accounts office for one top-class water buffalo.

CONJUGAL RITES

As a modern Torajan, Johannis sometimes displayed a curious prudery. The matter first came to prominence in the case of underwear, 'inner clothes'. Indonesian men favour stout, classical undergarments that are sturdy and capacious. My own 'inner clothes' having suffered in the course of my stay, I consulted Johannis about the possibility of securing fresh supplies. The matter, it seemed, was infinitely difficult and delicate. Most were sold in the market but by women. It was therefore out of the question for me to buy them there. They would giggle, ask questions about size and cover their noses. He could not ask a female relative to buy inner garments for me because I would be obliged to go into unseemly detail about just how 'inner' they would be.

Fortunately, he had a male friend who might help. Under cover of darkness, we made our way to a small shop on the outskirts of town. After a whispered conversation I was allowed to inspect and purchase several pairs which were rapidly rolled up to disguise their shape and wrapped in copious layers of newspaper. We scuttled back with the furtive haste of drug dealers. So great was the sense of some huge favour being done me that I had not dared haggle about the price.

The matter surfaced again in the village. One morning, I was woken by a very agitated Johannis who waved 'inner wear' at me in great outrage. I had washed the offending articles the day before and hung them on the washing line in front of the house. I should have hung them *behind* the house where only members of the family could see them.

But worse was to follow. Johannis's cousin, the somewhat simple but good-natured man who lived next door, was undone by a mixture of inner wear and bamboo.

The day after the festival, we were disturbed by voices from next door raised in anger. A woman seemed to be doing most of the talking or, in this case, shouting. Johannis promptly made for the kitchen to be able to hear better and stood with one ear pressed to the flimsy partition, grinning and nodding, infuriatingly unwilling to translate. Finally, he consented to do so with great glee. It appeared that the cousin had been detected, after drinking much palm-wine, heading for the bamboo with another woman from the village. The lady was of bad reputation. Her mother had been friendly with Japanese soldiers during the war. She was rumoured to have a Japanese father. The cousin's voice growled short, shifty answers, the voice of a man caught out. Far from turning away wrath, his demeanour seemed to drive his wife to a new frenzy of outrage. There was a long period of screaming followed by the unmistakable sound of a blow being struck, then – abruptly – silence.

The next day, the cousin ate with us. His wife had gone back to her parents. It was unthinkable that a man would cook for himself. No one was in any doubt about what would happen. The man would have to go to the wife and eat humble pie until either she agreed to come back or her family made her. It came as no surprise, therefore, when the cousin disappeared for a couple of days. Contrary to expectation, however, when he returned he was alone and in a very bad mood. No one dared ask about the wife. Occasionally he would try to rouse my interest in an expedition across the mountains to Makki where they still made cloth. It was difficult country and we would have to sleep in the forest. There were many leeches. I thought of the horse-ride from Mamasa and prevaricated.

Suddenly, however, the wife returned. Now it was she who was in a bad mood while he smirked and strutted around the village with the bravado of a fighting cock. He, after all, had the upper hand. Her family had sent her back.

Near the public washing place was a small coffee shop, a staging-post on the way to the outside world. Here, men would often gather to play cards, drink coffee or engage in conversation with the deaf-mute son of the house through gesture. Every village in Toraja seems to have its deaf-mute. No one seems to teach them sign language. The cousin was a hardened card-player and often to be found here.

One of the jobs of a chaste and dutiful spouse is to do the washing, including her husband's 'inner wear'. It therefore came as no surprise that the wronged wife appeared with the washing while the cousin idled in the coffee shop. The deaf-mute gasped and pointed. The cousin smirked at his cronies and played his cards with just a little more panache than usual. The wife began on the washing and laid out his underwear on the rocks. Still he smirked down at her. She fixed back her hair and looked up at him. Then, seizing a large rock and humming to herself, she began pounding the crotches of his underpants one by one. The cronies roared with gleeful malice. The deaf-mute gurgled rapturously. She had returned to wifely duty but still managed to have the last word. The cousin's sufferings did not end here, however. Johannis had now marked him down as a man ripe to be the butt of his humour.

Johannis, like many Christians, had a particular taste for the more bizarre manifestations of occult powers. Christianity, in its Torajan compromise with the old way, in no sense opposed the belief in spirits of nature, ghosts and hidden powers. His knowledge of such things was wild and approximate and quite often he would lead me on wild-goose chases. Sometimes this was not his fault. Anthropology is full of false trails.

On one occasion, I had shown interest in a particular kind of priest called *to burake tambolang*. This figure is associated with the east and fertility and has an odd sexual status, being a hermaphrodite, bisexual or transvestite – Torajans seem unclear about the distinctions. In Baruppu' such figures were regarded as an exoticism, though Nenek himself was properly referred to as *indo' aluk*, 'mother of tradition', and he was unable to explain this female appellation. Nenek was clear on the subject of the *tambolang*, however.

'They are male but they cannot have children because their member is very small. They have high voices. The *tambolang* is the only man who may enter a rice-barn.' That was particularly interesting since I had entered one that day. Nenek waved me away. 'Oh *you*. You do not matter. You are a puttyman, therefore strange. Anyway that was in the old days. Nowadays women run away, they are no good. If a man is not to starve, he has to go up there and get food.'

According to the literature, such figures no longer existed. I was particularly interested, therefore, when Johannis insisted he knew of one in Rantepao and took me there.

The man in question was very thin and old. His house swarmed with dogs and children. I sidled up to the matter gently. I was interested in the old ways and had been told that his family knew such things. He assented. Did he perhaps know anything about the *to burake tambolang?* There was a silence. He was embarrassed. 'Who's been talking to you?' he demanded, glaring at Johannis. 'That was my father. I know nothing about it.' He was distinctly peeved. 'I don't want to talk about it. I have retained nothing at all of all that from my father – except one thing.'

'What is that?'

'A taste for chocolate.'

I had been pleased anyway. If his father had been *tambolang* that seemed to settle the matter of his maleness. Johannis, however, was ready to torpedo my certainties.

'Don't forget, very many Torajans are adopted. We are always taking each other's children.' So I had learned nothing.

Johannis, too, had led me to the man in Baruppu' who – he claimed – could take buffalo horns from outside his house and make them fight each other as their living owners had done. I asked the man about it. He looked at me as though I were a madman and gently explained that when a buffalo was dead it was dead. Part of being dead was not moving any more. He stared at me as though fearing I might be dangerous.

'He was shy,' declared Johannis unabashed. 'Anyway, he will just think you are a schoolteacher driven mad by your learning.'

Neither of these incidents reflected any discredit on Johannis. Another event did.

One day he appeared, grinning at me. 'When you hear this, you will be happy,' he said. I looked suspicious. 'There is a special ceremony next door tonight.'

'What sort of ceremony?' He looked bashful and stared at his feet as he flexed his toes.

'It's something I've arranged.' Now I really was suspicious.

'It's something from the old days. You see, often when a man has a lot of bad luck he goes to an expert who tells him to make an offering to the central pillar of his house. I've persuaded my cousin next door to kill a chicken for the pillar and I will help with the ceremony.'

'*You* will help? Shouldn't Nenek do it?'

'Nenek doesn't want to. But he has told me how. I just thought you'd want to know. It's only next door.'

'Thank you.' I felt a sort of holy glow. My interest in the old ways seemed to be prompting a response in the heart of this young pagan.

'Ooh. One other thing. I'd like to write some notes on it. Can I have a pen, maybe one of those red waterproof ones?' Johannis had long admired these pens. An appeal to my pedagogic instinct.

'Of course.'

He popped the pen in his top pocket and went off humming.

That evening, we all assembled in the small ramshackle house. There were quite a number of young people there, friends of Johannis, and I had to squeeze in at the back. Johannis had arranged the set. The cousin was there, seated with his back to a large pillar, looking tense. Johannis and some of the other young bloods of the village sat around him in a circle. None of the old people had appeared. An oil lamp was turned very low so that it shone up into their faces from below, making them look strange and unearthly. There was a murmur of conversation. In front of the cousin was arranged a little fire with a small, round-bottomed clay pot standing on it. A knife and bits of wizened roots lay prepared. Johannis seemed to have assumed all the dignity of his grandfather. He rapped on the floor for silence, then began a choral song that the others joined in, sitting cross-legged and swaying their upper bodies back and forth. There was a little unseemly giggling. Johannis glared it into submission. The singing went on for some time. At a sign from Johannis, a small boy brought in a tiny white chick, gave it to him and scuttled away. Johannis held it aloft, waved it about and slit its throat. He sprinkled blood on the cousin's forehead, the pillar, the pot. One by one, ingredients were stirred into the brew. A foul odour pervaded the room like stale flatulence. Johannis appeared to be chanting like a *to minaa*.

Had Nenek taught him that? He began to make passes with his hands in the steam, gently running his fingers over the pot and up over his face, breathing in the steam. The cousin was exhorted to do the same, to inhale, to caress the pot, to rub the strength of it into his skin, to repeat the words. There was a sudden scream of laughter and someone turned up the lamp. All the young bloods roared and banged the floor. The cousin and I were left staring at each other in amazement. Then I saw what the cousin could not see. Johannis had smeared red ink from my pen all over the inside of the pot. Mixed with soot, it was now spread all over the face of his hapless victim. It was indelible. It took two days for him to get it off.

I should have been annoyed that my integrity had been impugned but my principal reaction was relief that Johannis had not chosen me as the victim.

Much as I wanted to remain in the village, it was time to return to the provincial capital. My visa would shortly expire and therefore had to be extended. It could all be arranged quite quickly, I was assured, at the Immigration Office. It took great stealth to leave the village without Nenek, who had set his heart on a jaunt to the city. The plan was that we would walk down the mountain, but we were unfortunate enough to meet up with the truck going in the same direction. Our previous crimes were now forgiven and we were urged to climb aboard. Reluctantly, we did so. We were even offered seats of honour in the cab. As soon as we reached the muddy section, the truck again became firmly stuck. For at least an hour we went through the same routine of digging, pushing, looking for rocks. Finally, Johannis nudged me. 'Let's walk,' he said.

Everyone stopped work to watch our treacherous departure. Johannis whistled. I hung my head.

It was a glorious day, fresh and clear. We encountered a man feeding long bundles of rushes to his buffalo, like planks into a circular saw. We walked together for a while and had a long discussion about what rituals a purchased buffalo could be used for as opposed to one raised at home. Twelve kilometres further on we reached the main road, where we might hope for a bus to the city. We sat by the coffee house and waited. We played with the children. We drank coffee. We cast water. We drank more coffee. The proprietor began to sound us out about a bed for the night. No buses came. The deranged schoolteacher appeared and began to tell me about his plans for industrial development. Suddenly, there was the sound of a bus. Johannis and I leapt to our feet, anxious lest it drive straight past. Round the corner came the truck that we had treacherously abandoned.

It was no time for false pride. Johannis waved them down and went into an enormously insincere performance of joy at their good fortune. The driver eyed us ruthlessly. Finally, it was agreed that we could get back on board. But we lost our seats in the front and we had to pay.

LET ME CALL YOU ...
PONG

The Immigration Office in Ujung Pandang was a hot, dusty concrete building down by the harbour. A long line of people sat waiting. They looked infinitely depressed as if they had all been waiting a long time and entertained no immediate hope of deliverance. There was no one behind the desk. Those waiting were sailors, straight from the naval academy. They were instantly friendly. I laughed at their passport photographs. They laughed at mine. I tried on their hats. They were all too small. After about an hour, six uniformed officials staggered in under the weight of an enormous, floppy chart. They spent the next forty minutes trying to fix it to the wall. The wall, however, proved to be solid concrete and resisted all efforts. Finally, they gave up and leant it in one corner. Only then could we see what it was. It was an immaculately lettered graph whose steeply rising curve showed 'Increasing Efficiency of the Office'.

We began by filling in forms. The sailors helped. Kindly, they explained that before even starting I would need to buy a dossier from a shop round the corner, otherwise no one would even process my application. 'The shop,' they whispered, 'is owned by the brother of the man behind the desk.' The shop took some finding. When I arrived back with my dossier, the office was closing. 'But it's only twelve o'clock.' The man shrugged. 'We open at eight tomorrow. But don't forget it's Friday. We close early so everyone can go to the mosque.'

By the following week, I had not made any great progress. The man dealing with my application was not inclined to be helpful.

'English?' he had said, smirking. 'When I went to England, the immigration people treated me like a dog. Yes, it's nice to have an English application.'

He sent me all round town three times on an extended paperchase. The hardest part was getting documentation from the head of the Ministry of Labour saying that I did not need any documentation from them. The sailors had similar problems. He made them buy patriotic stickers at enormous cost. By the end of the first week, their dossiers were covered with them. They exhorted sporting activities, family planning and care for the environment.

During one of the long lulls while my dossier was being 'processed', I paid a visit to the huge new university being built on the outskirts of the city to look up a man I had met briefly in England. I never found him, but by sheer good fortune I wandered into the office of an extremely elegant lady who taught English. In the course of conversation I described my difficulties at the Immigration Office. 'What is the man's name?'

'Arlen. He is a Batak – from Sumatra.'

'I do not think I know him. We are having a party at the hotel tonight,' she said. 'You must come.'

There are many hotels in Ujung Pandang but only one has any pretensions to luxury. It is built out over the sea with swaying palm-trees and waves that only make the politest of noises. A sign in the lobby informed me that I was present to say goodbye to a visiting American professor. As I entered, he shook me by the hand. 'I have greatly enjoyed working with you over the past two years,' he said with deep sincerity.

My hostess, Ibu Hussein, turned out to be the wife of the Dean. I was introduced to him, a rotund, smiling man who heaped my plate with food. The party was not at all like its English equivalent would have been. There were many speeches, mostly in English. One man with mad eyes and a tight blue suit gave a long address about his own stay in America, where he had learned to ride on the bus without paying and to extract many cans of Coca Cola from a machine for a single dime. Another man rose and with strong grievance announced that at *his* leaving party in America, he had been required to pay for his food. The Dean stood up and revealed that at one time he had studied in Manila, but there the bus drivers cheat the passengers, not the other way round. At that time he had been so poor that the only way he got enough to eat was to attend the receptions given every week for new Indonesian students. That meant he had to ride out to the airport on a bus just so that he could ride in again with the new batch. No one had ever recognized him. In America he had noticed that at the end of term the students stole all the clocks.

Some students, scrubbed and desperately shy, recited poems in an English that was quite incomprehensible. A young man stood up and indicated the departing professor. 'This man is my father. I very love him,' and began to cry. A haughty stray cat promenaded across the roof beams with infinite poise as the Dean began to sing 'Auld Lang Syne' in various languages. By far the most convincing was Japanese.

Johannis lived out in the Torajan area of the city, a delightful spot near a big pond surrounded by vegetable gardens. Its only disadvantage was the enormous number of mosquitoes there. Feeling in high good humour after the university reception, I decided to visit him and we went off to drink palm-wine with some of the other Torajans in the house. We sat in a large yard on rough wooden stools while the foaming bamboo tubes of wine belched and rumbled against the wall. After some time, a short, fat man made a dramatic entrance on a motorbike directly into the yard. Everyone went very quiet. 'Police,' muttered Johannis. The man sat on his motorbike, lit a cigarette and looked around.

'Who's the Dutchman?' he shouted. Johannis swivelled round reluctantly.

'A tourist, Pak. He's going to Toraja.'

'Get him over here.'

He looked me up and down. What was my name? Where was I staying? Why was I with these people? Didn't I know this was an illegal drinking place? These were bad people. I would get myself into trouble. I was a guest in his country. He would take me somewhere else to drink. I was about to protest but saw Johannis give me a significant look and shake his head. I climbed on the motorbike and off we went.

Our destination was another illegal drinking place. It cost me three beers and an hour's attention to the many wrongs he had suffered, in his village in Bali, in the police-force, from his wife.

'More drink,' he demanded. I felt it was time to try a big lie.

'I'm sorry. I have to get back. I have to see the governor tomorrow morning.' He looked at me. Could it be true? He doubted it but couldn't be sure and rolled off the bench on to his feet.

'Take you back to the hotel,' he slurred. 'Guest in the country.' We wove rather erratically back to the hot, depressing place where I was staying. I took my leave, thanking him for 'looking after me'.

'Hang on,' he said. 'Now there's a thing. I seem to be out of petrol. You wouldn't have a thousand rupiahs on you would you?' There seemed no point in changing my policy of craven appeasement now. I paid up.

'What's your name?' I asked, trying to give it the same inflection as you would if asking an English policeman his number.

'Venus,' he said. 'My name is Venus.'

Day after day, I went back to the Immigration Office. Sometimes Arlen was there and had new tasks for me to perform. Sometimes he was not there at all and I just waited. Then, on one extraordinary day, the door of the Office Head was flung open. I had tried several times to see this man and always been directed back to Arlen. He approached me with an air of deference, bowing and dancing on the balls of his feet.

'I hope,' he said, 'you are being looked after properly. Perhaps there is something I can do to help you?' It was hard to know where to start. He smiled ingratiatingly as I launched into an account of my difficulties. Five minutes later, I was leaving the office with a three-week extension. It had taken twelve days. The Office Head opened the door for me.

'Please,' he said, 'send my regards to Ibu Hussein.'

I phoned the university and got through to the Dean.

'Ah,' he sighed, 'he was not supposed to say anything. My wife *did* happen to pass through the Immigration Office this morning. You see, it just so happens that the Office Head is a student at the university. To get promotion, he needs to pass an examination. At the moment he is finding the course *very* hard. Perhaps, if the processing of visas took less time, he would have more time for his studies and the course would not seem quite so hard.'

'I see. How can I ever thank you?'

'There is no need. Many people in England have been nice to me, so I am nice to you. Perhaps in the future you will be able to be nice to an Indonesian.'

When I returned to the hotel, I found the door to my room ajar. Voices could be heard from inside. My heart sank. It was obviously the English Club who had tracked me down and would make my life hideous with their irregular verbs. Still, I had to be nice to an Indonesian. With a set smile, I opened the door. It was the sailors from the Immigration Office.

'We got your address from the form,' they announced, 'and told the people here we were all your cousins. We have come to see you in case you are lonely and sad.'

I told them of the extraordinary events with my visa. They smiled and hugged me. Surely I could not be that lovable?

'Then you can come with us to see the butterflies.' Oh dear! I thought of the zoo in Surabaya. I was doomed to undertake a dreary crawl through the fleshpots of the old town.

'My wife would not like it.'

'She would prefer you sit here sadly rather than come with us and see the beautiful butterflies? That cannot be.' See? Perhaps my participation would be limited to a voyeur's role.

'It is only ten o'clock in the morning. They won't be up.'

They nodded earnestly. 'They rise very early. It is the best time before they get hot and tired. Besides, we have borrowed a truck just for you.' It was true. Parked outside was a truck in the blue livery of the Indonesian navy. There was nothing for it. I owed an Indonesian a kindness. I went.

It came as a considerable relief when we drew up outside a butterfly sanctuary. We spent a delightful day sipping warm orange squash and looking at pretty Lepidoptera. It was quite unlike a day out with English tars.

We arrived back at sunset.

'You will come to our house near the biscuit factory.' Seven of them lived in a tiny hut covered with pictures of an American pop-singer. 'We like her because she is a virgin. She sings about it,' they explained.

'But how do you all sleep here? You cannot all lie down?'

'We take it in turns. Some sleep till two in the morning, then they have to go outside so others can lie down. Bruno sleeps during the day too but then he is from Irian Jaya.' Bruno grinned a huge black man's grin.

As the sun set and warm dust blew around our feet we chewed on broken biscuits bought cheap from the factory next door. Never before or since have I felt such warm companionship.

The more I thought about the trek through the forest to Makki – suggested by Johannis's luckless cousin – the less I felt inclined to undertake it. Yet it was here that traditional weavers were to be found. Fortunately, there was an alternative. A well-known Torajan weaver had recently moved from Kalumpang to the town of Mamuju. With a bit of luck, if I left at dawn, I could probably get there by bus in a single day.

In retrospect, the journey has an unreal, nightmarish quality. Indonesians are excellent drivers. They have to be to do the things they do and survive. There were two near-accidents, when a horse bolted out of a side-road and when a buffalo ran into the side of our tiny crammed van, which was speeding along the narrow strip of tarmac. Then there was a third incident in which a deaf woman stepped out into our path. At such moments time is slowed down. There was somehow plenty of opportunity to scream and point out the woman only inches in front of us and time for the driver to swerve into a deep drainage ditch and rocket out again scattering a group of schoolchildren whose terrified faces blew against the windscreen like leaves. Miraculously, no one was hurt but the clutch had been torn out from under the vehicle. This being Indonesia, however, it was not a matter of two weeks in a garage. The driver calmly sat down, lit a fire and reforged the damaged parts so that within two hours we were off again.

On either side were lush rice-fields giving five crops of rice every two years. Prosperous-looking houses were going up everywhere. Gleaming new mosques clearly showed we were in a Buginese area, among the pushy Muslim seafarers who have established themselves in many of the littoral areas of the archipelago. The roads were dotted with tiny carts pulled by chubby horses. Apart from the mosques, it looked like an American notion of the good, simple life.

Presently the road began to hug the shore. I could not understand why the area had not been mentioned in any guidebook. Golden sands fringed a limpid blue sea. Simple wooden houses with balconies stood out over the waves while fishermen mended nets and women wove. Naked brown children laughed and sported in the pools. Dramatic outcrops of rock threw flying buttresses up into the cloudless sky. I began to imagine Mamuju with mounting excitement. The hotel would be a large white building of wood with a veranda from which I could watch the glory of a tropical sunset. The menu would be a riot of seafood. A landlubber's fantasy.

Things started to go wrong quite quickly after that. As we drove deeper into Buginese territory, a sort of Muslim detestation of dogs seemed to grip the driver. He swung the van in great arcs at those sitting harmlessly by the roadside and finally achieved a certainly fatal hit on a puppy. He grinned at the passengers, several of whom were muttering against him.

'Dogs are unclean,' he said.

Perhaps it is more than chance that lack of fluency and theological weakness conspire to make one sound like the Bible. 'Even unclean beasts are made by God and the man who kills them is a fool' Had I *really* said that? The driver pouted and sulked. Possibly it was this that led him to declare his unwillingness to take us further than the next town without extra payment – though the reasons he invoked were the lateness of the hour and the unpredictable state of the road.

I was not inclined to spend the night in the town of Majene. It was doubtless well enough in its own way but could not compare with the delights of Mamuju as pictured in my own imagination. After wandering round the market for some time, I finally found a man who was bound for Mamuju that very night. Alas, he only had a flat pick-up truck and the cab was fully occupied but I was welcome for modest payment to travel on the back. It was a beautiful evening of mellow sunshine. Mamuju was only a hundred kilometres away. It would be a joy.

To my considerable embarrassment, I was not permitted to simply huddle down at the rear. A cane chair was installed on the platform and I was required to sit on it in a very upright pose like a colonial governor in state. The man drove with solemn precision, pausing lavishly at intersections as though wishing the maximum possible number of people to see me.

It was in some ways unfortunate that this was the day on which pilgrims return from the journey to Mecca, sporting the white turbans of their Haji status in a procession through the streets. The roads were lined with expectant crowds, craning their necks, waiting impatiently for the arrival of their loved ones who had been raised to new heights of piety by their onerous journey. It was a day when personal transformations were expected, when sinners might return as saints, when close relatives might be rendered almost unrecognizable through their contact with the holy. The ceremonial pace of the truck served to associate it with such a procession. As we advanced, a devout murmur went up, cut short with screams of hysterical laughter at the moment I became visible in my high chair. The absurd deflation of his expectation caused one man to fall off his veranda in astonishment, while another dropped the teapot he was holding as though its searing heat had just penetrated to his fingers. Whenever we halted at junctions, cheering, laughing crowds would rush up good-naturedly. They gently squeezed my arm and spoke the only English they knew. 'Yes,' they whispered. 'Yes.'

This imperial progress continued until darkness fell and we approached the town of Mamuju. People retreated into their houses to avoid a blanket of mosquitoes that seemed to drop from the sky. The road was obscured by dense clouds of smoke as they fired piles of coconut husks under the house to drive away the insects. It might be thought difficult for mosquitoes to pursue a man travelling on the back of a truck but they managed it. They wormed and bit and itched until I too was forced to smoke to lessen their attentions.

There is no way to explain Mamuju except as a deliberate insult to the beauty of the rest of the coast. On seeing it I began to wish I had braved the forest leeches. It is an ill-natured bunch of sleazy concrete dwellings gathered around a dust-bowl. The centre of the town is an enormous heap of decaying refuse on which food markets are perilously erected. It must once have had a fine beach but now this is covered with concrete slabs on which more refuse is dumped so that goats can feed there. Several years ago, an earthquake damaged the water pipes and large areas of the town are still cut off from any regular supply. The dingy hotel was appallingly hot and simply had no water at all. Holes had been poked in the thin cardboard partitions between the rooms to allow neighbours to inspect each other illicitly. The only food available in town was a greasy stew of fishheads. I tossed and turned through a sleepless night of further mosquito attack and, as soon as it was light, fled to the Torajan part of town.

Ethnic identity in such areas is largely religious. If you are Muslim, you are Buginese, if Christian, Torajan. A Torajan who becomes Muslim is often not recognized as Torajan any more. An air of brooding religious confrontation pervades the atmosphere.

The Torajan settlements were clustered round their churches and it was here that I found Aneka, the woman I had come to seek. As an introduction I brought with me a letter I had been given by a Baruppu' woman, Aneka's daughter. Aneka was a woman in her mid-forties, worn and tight-lipped. She read the letter and invited me to stay. 'We can read the Bible together,' she offered. Like Johannis's mother, she was a convert to Christianity and it assumed a prominent position in the forefront of her life. That was fine by me. Most of the languages I have ever learnt began with the appropriate Bible translation. Often the Bible would be the only book ever printed in that tongue.

She and her husband had adopted a curious, pious pidgin so that the announcement of anything had always began, 'It is God's will that ...' whereas the announcement of anything good began, 'God has opened the way so that ...' One rapidly adopts such locutions. When, on the third day, the husband asked me whether I was going outside to 'cast large water', I replied with no conscious comic intention, 'If God opens the way.'

Despite her religious apostasy, Aneka seemed initially a wholly traditional weaver, mistress of the lengthy process whereby a bundle of white fluff collected from her cotton bushes was transformed into beautiful blue and red textiles. Between long bouts of reading the Bible, she eagerly demonstrated the preparation of dyes from plants. I noted that she used nearly two litres of chilli to fix the colour of a small cloth – which explained my reaction to the blanket on the Mamasa trail. The cloths, known as *sarita* and *seko mandi,* are of great importance for festivals all over Torajaland and are used to ornament people and buildings. Special powers – putting out fires, predicting dire events – are attributed to particular cloths, and they rapidly become heirlooms.

They are made by a relatively simple process whereby the

warp threads are stretched out on a frame and parts are blanked off with plastic string. Dye is then painted over the whole. When it is dry, part of the protective string is removed and the process repeated with other colours. The threads are divided in two and woven into two cloths which are then sewn together to form a single textile made of two identical sections. The end result is a thick, soft material richly ornamented with glowing colours that gently mellow over the years. Of particular interest was the fact that some of the designs used in woodcarving also turn up in the cloths. Aneka gave them the same names as Nenek had, but whereas she maintained that carving designs had been copied from textiles, Nenek attributed primacy in the opposite direction. For him, carving designs dropped directly from Heaven ready-made. For Aneka, they had been invented by women like herself. Perhaps it was this that had encouraged her recently to innovate. In discussions of such matters, scholars tend to opt for one or other as the original source, ignoring the fact that there is at least a third term in the relationship – the designs of tattooing that are nowadays rapidly disappearing. She had started including crosses, sheep and other Christian symbols in experimental cloths that she was as yet too nervous to show the world. Sheep particularly bothered her, since she was not sure she had ever seen an authentic example. It is surprising how often they are mentioned in the Bible.

It took nearly a week to see the whole process of cloth-making. It was with a definite feeling of liberation, that I climbed aboard the bus that would take me back to Torajaland, a large bundle of Aneka's cloths stowed under my feet. Soon, however, they were removed to make way for coconuts and used as a seat for a tiny spiky-haired child who stared at me with eyes of deep wonder.

A podgy man was installed beside the driver with elaborate

displays of deference. He was called Bapak a lot. Clearly a man of some standing. We watched resentfully as his own space was carefully preserved from incursion while more and more passengers were crammed into ours. Finally, the driver appeared at the side window and made gestures, albeit deferential, that he should move up to allow another in. Bapak puffed and tutted fretfully. We smirked. His bastion was breached. The door opened and one of the most beautiful girls I have ever seen climbed in beside him. He turned round and leered at us.

The bus shot off, coconuts rumbling around our feet. The child still stared at me with wonder as its mother pushed handfuls of rice into its mouth.

Outside the first town, we were waved to a halt by a policeman with a rifle. A guilty hush settled over the bus. The policeman took his time. He eyed the bus up and down. He walked round it. He took off his sunglasses. He beckoned the driver outside with his rifle, stuck his thumbs in his belt and embarked on a lengthy oration. Words blew in through the window, '... danger to passengers ... respect for the law ... integrity of the Republic'. The driver hung his head. We all sat to attention.

'Two passengers too many,' said Bapak. 'He speaks in high principles. This will be expensive.'

The lecture continued for several minutes more. The policeman embarked on a thorough examination of the vehicle – lights, tyres – and demanded sheaves of documentation. Then, he led the driver round the back.

'That's a good sign,' said Bapak nodding.

The driver could be heard saying, 'Yes, Pak. But I think *just this once* it might be overlooked

He got back in cocky and grinning and started the engine.

'How much?' asked Bapak.

'Two thousand, but he didn't even notice the licence I gave

him isn't mine.' He laughed and slammed the bus into gear.

Round the next corner, two more passengers waved the bus down and got on. Normal service resumed.

Much of the journey was spent dozing. I surfaced briefly later that night and saw a mountain gleaming in the moonlight. I recognized it at once. The young Torajan next to me was awake.

'Isn't that,' I asked, 'the mountain where there was the ladder that linked heaven and earth in the days of the ancestors?'

He looked at it and shrugged indifferently. 'Maybe. But we call it porno mountain. If you look at the rocks, there is the male and there the female ...!'

Arriving in Rantepao felt like coming home. There was the friendly, ugly town. There were the cheery, easy-going people. At the hotel, Johannis and a very tall, thin man were asleep in a chair, leaning on each other, their mouths open. It did my heart good to see them.

The name of Johannis's friend was Bismarck. I yearned to introduce him to Hitler but I suppose they would not have seen the point. According to his own accounts, Bismarck had led a life of high adventure. He was a member of the Torajan nobility or as he put it, 'gold class.' This was apparent in his bearing. When talking to non-Torajans he was easy and relaxed. When Torajans spoke to him, he was instantly stiff and referred to them in the third person or simply ignored them completely.

At one time he had dealt in illegal substances in Jakarta, then imported pornography through foreign friends, but he had eventually been consumed by self-disgust and returned to Toraja where he spent as much time as possible in the forest. He was now a dealer in 'stolen' antiquities, but seemed genuinely to pursue his calling with high moral sentiments.

'It is like this,' he explained. 'The people who come here are willing to pay a million rupiahs for a grave figure. Imagine how much that means to a simple farmer. His children can go to school and have a future. He will have security. He is probably a Christian and sees grave figures as a bad thing. If he is a pagan, he can sell the old figure and buy a new one and still have a good profit. Even the ancestors agree. They are always asked. Everyone is happy. But the government has forbidden it because they fear that if the figures are sold tourists will no longer come. So the family will arrange for the figures to be 'stolen' and they will be sold in Bali or London. They come to me because I have contacts. I do not go to them. They know my family and trust me. I take a percentage and see they are not cheated. *Always,* I insist they wait one month after they have decided to sell just in case they change their minds. Often I sell to museums. Maybe your museum would not buy but American museums do. I have many friends in American museums. Anyway, I think you are probably all the same. You want to take the beautiful things and put them in a box and send them away. Now, would you like to go to my house and I will show you some fine things.'

'I would love to see them but you know I cannot buy them. Anything over fifty years old requires a permit. That is the law.'

'Yes, that is the law, But come and see. I like to show things to people who enjoy them.'

His house was a treasury of old and strange objects, spinning wheels, doors, hats, shoes. He demonstrated them all with enormous pride. He put on a prince's hat and sat in dignity, seized a spear and became a warrior, pulled out an areca-nut container and chewed like an old villager. In the midst of his performance his tiny daughter appeared in a fluffy pink party frock and a gold paper crown. They looked at each other and laughed.

'Ah yes. She is going to a birthday party.' Bismarck took her on his knees, eyes full of love.

'One day,' he said to me, 'you and I will walk the hills together.

I will take you to places no one else knows about. I feel it in my bones. I am not wrong about these things. I have seen the Lord of the Forest.'

'The Lord of the Forest?'

'Yes. You will not find him in any of your anthropology books about the religion of the Torajans but in the villages we all know him. I, who was brought up a Christian, have met him. That is one of the reasons I have gone back to the old ways.'

'How did it happen?'

'Well, I will tell you. I wanted to meet him just to see if he really existed. I went into the deep forest for three nights and I just sat naked and waited. The first night I had been drinking and nothing happened. The second night I had eaten normally. On the third night, I had fasted. Suddenly he was there.'

'What was he like?'

'A very old man. There was no bottom half to his body. He floated on mist and he spoke to me. "What do you want?" he said. I said, "Nothing. I just wanted to see that you were real." Imagine.' He struck himself on the forehead. 'I could be a rich man now if I had said the right thing, but I just wanted to know. "Do not worry," he said. "I will always look after you in my forest." Then he was gone. *Then,* quite suddenly I was frightened.' Bismarck laughed. 'I ran out of the trees as fast as I could and hid in the house and shook with fear. But now, you see, I am strong because I know for sure.'

There came an odd scratching noise outside. Putting down his daughter, Bismarck went to the door and there was a murmur of conversation. He returned laughing.

'There is an old man there, asking for you. He asked for "Pong Bali" – *Pong* is like *puang*. It is our word for "lord". So now we have a name for you – Pong Bali. Don't worry. It is not the Lord of the Forest.'

I went outside. It was Nenek. He refused to come in. It would not be proper. This was the house of a noble and he was suddenly shy. He had walked the thirty-odd kilometres to town to buy areca-nut but had no money. Perhaps I would give him some? The simplicity of the thought made it irresistible. But something else was troubling him.

'I have not been able to sleep. I have promised you one buffalo. But someone in the village said one buffalo would not even pay the cost of a ticket to England.'

'Nenek, one buffalo is for *you*. We would have to pay for your ticket and look after you there.'

An expression of relief swept over his face. When were we going to England? If it was immediately, he would need to buy quite a lot of areca-nut.

'That,' said Bismarck with authority, watching him go, 'is a good old man. You are working with him?'

I told him about the exhibition.

'I am delighted. For once, the people who make things will get the money, not crooks and dealers like me. I have a big house here, lots of land. If you need help or want to store things, I will help. No charge.'

I found it hard to think of Bismarck as a crook. Perhaps, on second thoughts, he did have very little to do with Hitler.

Johannis and I returned to Baruppu' and found not only that Nenek had returned but that his daughter had too. She bore all the marks I had come to recognize of a Christian Torajan worthy woman. Nenek and I would wander away from her somewhat heavy virtue and talk about the old ways. In the evenings we would play a sort of party game where he and his neighbours would dig out their old heirlooms or even old everyday objects and talk about them.

Nenek was particularly proud of his tall pedestal rice-dish, standing some three feet tall, the stem of bleached buffalo bone that was the prerogative of a *to minaa*. Another man had beautiful wooden vegetable dishes carved with buffalo heads. Others had old swords and cloths.

'These are not toys,' explained Nenek. 'They bring wealth to a house. We need them for festivals.' He had a cautionary tale about ancient cloth that had been sold and brought misfortune to all until it was returned to the house where it belonged. He brought out a square of very soft, very thick fur with two cords attached. 'What is this?'

I turned it all ways. Johannis prodded quizzically at it. A grin split his face. 'I know.' He placed it delicately on his head like a toupee and tied the strings. Nenek and his cronies rocked on their heels with delight. In a single smooth movement, Nenek snatched it off his head, tucked it under his buttocks and sat down.

'In the old days, Torajans only had rocks to sit on. So we used these.' He pulled out another strange thing, long and pointed with bulbous swellings at either end. It was made of bone or very hard wood. It looked a little like one of those mushroom-shaped objects that women used to use for darning socks. I shook my head. Again Johannis leaped in.

'It is used for mending the holes in socks.' Nenek and I laughed at such a naive thought.

It was, Nenek explained in a low voice, the Torajans' secret weapon against Buginese men. Johannis and I looked at each other blankly, while Nenek was delighted by our puzzlement. He explained, cackling, that it was a penis-bar, inserted crosswise in the male member and drove Torajan women wild with delight. This was the reason that any Torajan women who slept with a local man in the old days, would never look at Buginese men even with their long noses. Johannis went silent and looked thoughtful.

I was surprised to learn that Nenek had a wife in another part of the village.

'We don't live together any more,' said Nenek. 'She became a Christian. All my children have become Christians. I am the last one left. But they keep going on at me. I say I was born in this religion and I will die in this religion.'

Nenek seemed to have been undermined by a surprising tolerance. 'They get this religion from school,' he declared. 'If it wasn't for school no one would change, but it's good too. Without school, we would all be ignorant like in the old days.'

It was sad to think that when he died the old religion would die in Baruppu' too. There was no one left who wanted to undergo the burden of committing to memory the thousands of lines of verse that constitute the knowledge of a priest. It was hard not to cast Nenek in the role of an embattled bastion of tradition. Yet he was someone who had engaged the modern world. At one time he had been a dealer in coffee. During the Japanese occupation, he had hidden Chinese Indonesians in the village. He had learnt to speak Indonesian and to read and write by sending grandchildren to school and making them tell him, at the end of each day, what they had learned. He had taken what he wanted from the modern world and left the rest. But Torajaland was a place where the self-evident opposition between traditional and modern was difficult to maintain. It was income from modern tourism and jobs in the Indonesian state that fuelled the ritual inflation that seemed to be going on all over the area. People who would not have been permitted sumptuous funerals in the old days were investing in them now, converting their cash into status – rather as nineteenth-century English industrialists spent their fortunes on ruinous country estates. Even a Christian funeral required the presence of a *to minaa* whose traditional wisdom would be chanted through a loudspeaker. Yet when I mentioned my plan of taking Nenek to

London to the village head, he was aghast.

'You can't possibly,' he said. 'It's not fair. He hasn't even been to school. *I* have. I know the names of almost all the railway stations in Holland.'

The next time I saw him I asked, 'What would happen, Nenek, if you went to England? No one could declare the time for death ceremonies. No one could tell them when they could start building houses again.'

He laughed. 'That's no problem. In the old days we did it by the stars not the calendar. I'm the one who decides when the stars are right. I can do it when I like. Let's just go. My body is old but my heart is young. I love new things.'

It was time to take my leave. I had managed to extend my visa once. I would not be able to do so again. Nenek and Johannis saw me to the end of the valley. Torajans are uninhibited weepers and we were all the worse for tears.

'If Nenek comes, Johannis, you must come too.'

He grinned. 'If God opens the way.'

With the corniness that only deity or Hollywood allow, there was a beautiful rainbow over the valley.

'That means good luck,' said Nenek.

I wondered whether I would ever see them again.

THE RETURN MATCH

For once, my pessimism was misplaced. It took only two years and five visits to Sulawesi to get every stick and twig of the materials necessary to construct a rice-barn back to London. The shipment included rocks to be ground into paint, rattan for the roof and the largest pile of bamboo I have ever seen. Only then was it possible to bring over four carvers to build it inside a gallery of the Museum of Mankind in the heart of the city. It was surprisingly difficult to ensure that it would neither fall through the floor (people do not usually weigh rice-barns) nor extend upwards through the ceiling. There were some very low points along the way.

When I first returned with the exciting news that the project was on, Nenek failed totally to recognize me. In my mind I had often imagined this scene. He would, of course, cry. Probably so would I. But a year had passed since we met and all putty-men look the same.

'I cannot possibly go with you to London. Last year, there was an odd Dutchman who came. I promised I would go with *him*.'

Another bad moment was when the trucker who was supposed to bring materials from the village to Rantepao attempted to renegotiate the contract en route and ended up by dumping everything by the roadside. It became a matter of desperate urgency to get it moved before the first rains came. By then, difficulties had compounded themselves to the point where I arrived in Ujung Pandang with two enormous lorries of wood, nowhere to store them, a ship due to sail the next day and no money to pay anyone. Before we could embark material, it had to be inspected and documented three times. We ended up, in the rain, at ten at night, with the entire shipment spread out in the road, trying to photograph it in the dark. A minibus drew up and from it sprang Nenek with as much sprightliness as his seventy-odd years could muster.

'I have come to help unload the wood,' he announced. 'Are we leaving for England now?'

The only factor that triumphed over all these difficulties was the astonishing helpfulness of ordinary Torajans. They helped not because they were being paid or because it was their job to do so, but because they saw I needed help. The final blow was the devaluation of the Indonesian currency in the midst of the operation which, far from being an unexpected windfall, nearly wrecked everything as all banks refused to change money for some two weeks. It was typical of the Torajan hotelier that when I explained my total absence of funds and my need to leave without paying, he simply shrugged. 'I know you will send me the money as soon as you can.'

Personal documentation had been a major difficulty. It is very hard to get travel papers for a man who does not even know how old he is. The forms that needed to be filled in seemed perversely ill-adapted to carvers living up a mountain in Indonesia. Telephone number? Educational certificates? Income in money? Even remembering names and ages of all children defeated the younger men. They worked out that one had eight children and one seven, but did not know their ages or even relative order of birth. That was the sort of thing only women knew.

Nenek made matters worse by changing his mind half-way

about who should accompany him, so that when I returned to Baruppu' the village was split into warring factions, each of which felt it had been wronged and expected me to put matters right. Then there were predictable hitches. It is always awkward to get spears and swords on to jet aircraft, yet they were part of Nenek's priestly outfit and he would not be parted from them. Less predictable were problems in Java, where the word *Nenek* can only be used of aged females and the Immigration Department were ill-prepared for a man to be so called.

Nevertheless, quite suddenly, they were here in an English 'hot season' with the wind and rain howling outside the house. It seemed only fair that, as I stayed with them in Torajaland, they would stay with me in England.

The carvers were like a history of Torajaland in miniature. Nenek, in his seventies, was a high priest of the old religion and was in overall charge. Tanduk, a large affable Christian in his early forties, would do most of the heavy woodwork. Karre, an irascible Christian in his mid-thirties would do most of the carving and the roof. With some justification, he was known as 'the buffalo'. Johannis, now a student of English and a modern pagan, would be a channel of communication and general link-man.

From the start, they were amazingly adaptable. As carvers, they were used to the idea of working away from their homes and families. Johannis was the only one who had lived in the city, but Nenek had already once experienced an aeroplane and loved it. Technological toys held little wonder for them. It is true that they were amazed that English telephones would permit people to speak to each other in Indonesian and never tired of using them. Central heating they adored, as do I – I had had it put in in preparation for their coming. But it is always true that electronic gadgets, which cannot possibly be understood by a layman but must simply be accepted, cause less sustained speculation than human abilities. They, who had come to astonish the English with woodworking craft, were fascinated by bricklaying on building sites – the speed, the economy of movement of skilled workers. It was always difficult to get Nenek past a building going up. He would stride amongst the brickwork asking questions. 'What's this?' 'Why do they do that?' 'How much does a crane cost?'

The problem with some novelties lay precisely in their being assimilated to something Indonesian that they already knew. While it is normal to stand in an Indonesian bathroom and simply throw water all over yourself, in an English bathroom the consequences can be disastrous. While there was no problem about turning taps *on*, they would never remember to turn them *off*, since in Torajaland, water simply gushes eternally from a bamboo pipe. They never quite believed me when I told them it was safe to drink the water from the tap without boiling it and furtively continued to take their own precautions.

I confess to taking a certain pleasure in noting that they found it as impossible to cross an English road as I did an Indonesian one, but rapidly found that I was developing the paranoia of a parent. I found myself planning routes so that they crossed as few roads as possible and noting pivoting paving slabs so that I could warn Nenek against them. The smallest journey became a nightmare of imagined dangers and snares for their unwary feet. It sometimes seemed as though they had been sent exclusively to make me suffer what I had made my parents suffer as a child.

'Come and eat!' I would say. 'Yes,' they would reply. Fifteen minutes later, they were still sitting carving.

'In ten minutes we must leave,' I would warn them. But when we tried to get through the door they would still be in sarongs watching television.

In the early years of this century, the American anthropologist

Boas took some Kwakiutl Indians to New York. Apparently, they were unimpressed by the tall buildings and cars. The only things that struck them were bearded ladies in Times Square and the knobs on the ends of banisters in lodging houses. It is impossible to predict what people from another culture will find remarkable.

The first shock for them was that all British were not white. West Indians look to them like Irian Jayans, the Indonesian half of New Guinea, so they tended to expect them to talk Indonesian. Chinatown did not surprise them. 'Chinese are good at business. They get everywhere.' Indians they would assume to be Arabs. The most mortifying experience was to discover that there is no slot 'Indonesian' in English folk categories and that they themselves would be regarded as Chinese.

A second shock was that all Europeans were not rich. Admittedly, they had seen young puttypersons in Torajaland playing at being poor, but everyone knew they would be carrying larger sums of money than a Torajan farmer would see in a lifetime. Why did I have no servants, no car and chauffeur? They were distressed by the drunks who roam the streets of London, being unused to situations where you pretend that people shouting at you are not there. That people should have no work and receive money from the government staggered them like right-wing Tories. Surely they had misunderstood? Were these people not pensioners? Had they not at some time been in the army and were receiving money for their wounds?

They arrived at a moment of high political activity, just days before a General Election, and were amazed at the lack of respect we show politicians. 'We would go to jail for that!' was their constant cry. Yet it should not be assumed that they envied us our freedom. To them, it appeared more as lack of order, as messy and reprehensible ill-management. Johannis summed it up swiftly. 'I see that England is a place where no one respects anyone.'

The position of the Queen puzzled them too. Like many foreigners they found it hard to imagine the relationship between a female prime minister and a female sovereign and drew the inevitable conclusion that only women are eligible for positions of power in this strange land. 'It is like the Minang people of Sumatera,' they opined with appropriate ethnographic example. 'There it is the women who own everything and the poor men are sent abroad to work for them. You are just like them. We are sorry for you.'

The offices of sovereign and prime minister became confused. They kept asking why the Queen had not stood for political office. It also worried them that I did not have her picture on the wall as, in Indonesia, one would have the President's portrait.

Certain concessions had been made towards the Torajan way of life. It would be easier for me to change than to ask them to. Beds were unpleasantly soft. They preferred mattresses on the floor. Instead of spreading themselves around the house, they all slept in one room. 'If we had a nightmare and slept alone, who would comfort us?' Spittoons were essential for Nenek's habit of chewing areca-nut. It is very hard to buy spittoons in London.

In their first few days, two things troubled them more than any other – the unearthly hush in which English people live, and lavatory paper. Where was the noise of cassette-players, honking traffic, street-pedlars, screaming children? They could not sleep at night. The only sounds were owls, always frightening, associated with witchcraft. To Torajans, a good house, a successful family, is characterized by bustle and children and the presence of a constant stream of visitors that would drive a Westerner mad. Eventually they took to playing pop-music very loudly till they fell asleep. As for lavatory paper, it was simply the most appalling thing they had ever heard of. They were deeply shocked by European lack of hygiene. 'English women look very attractive,' said Tanduk, 'but when I think of the lavatory paper and how dirty they are, it puts me off.'

In all this, our positions were suddenly, ludicrously reversed. I became *their* informant trying to explain my culture to their relentless probings. Not surprisingly, they often found my explanations inadequate. One element of the exhibition was a Torajan water-powered bird-scarer. As the water flows from level to level of the rice-terraces, it operates a clever pivoting mechanism that makes a loud noise. This is sufficient to frighten away birds and other predators. At the bottom of our version was a pool of water. Every day, people threw money into it. Nenek was intrigued by this. Why did they do it? Did they think an earth spirit lived in the pool? I was unable to enlighten him. 'They do it for luck,' or 'It is our custom,' – neither satisfied him. He would walk round the gallery every day to look at it and inquire the value of each coin, muttering his amazement. 'When I am old,' he said, shaking his grey locks, 'I shall come and live here and dig pools – so people can throw their money in.'

We travelled to the museum every morning by underground train. They liked that a lot and rapidly became masters of it. Fellow passengers were sometimes alarmed to see them climb on hugging pieces of wood they had insisted on carving at home the night before. Initially, Nenek had difficulties with escalators. Although he could run over a greasy log bridge in Torajaland, where I would have to get down and crawl, he found it hard to cope with staircases that moved or the motor skills involved in standing up in a moving train. It was only a matter of time until the source of the problem was tracked down. It was shoes. The wearing of shoes is the mark of formal dress in Indonesia – the equivalent of wearing a tie. Not to wear them at all, or just to wear sandals, is the sign of being a rustic. People who have gone much of their lives unshod have very broad feet and find it painful to cram their feet into shoes. Once Nenek had been persuaded not to wear them, he was able to walk much better and no longer teetered perilously on the escalators.

While they could all navigate in and out of work unaided, it was Johannis who was silently accorded the role of link-man with the outside world. *He* was expected to internalize the map of the underground, the techniques of using public telephones and ways of discouraging the attentions of drunks. On the second evening we lost him in Piccadilly in the crowds. A desperate search failed to trace him. When we arrived home he had returned before us, unaided, on the underground. I was impressed.

In their basic flexibility, only one thing, it seemed, was not negotiable. They had to have rice three times a day. Attempts to wean them on to other kinds of food via spaghetti or noodles failed. They would try alternatives with deep distaste, never complain but not eat them either. I soon abandoned all attempts to vary the diet. Potatoes and such like were acceptable but only as a supplement to rice, never as a substitute. This meant that days would begin about six o'clock in the morning with the boiling of rice. The three months of their stay are viewed through the steam of rice. A Western house is strangely ill-suited to rice. After a few weeks it blocked sinks, drains, stuck to the floor. Chicken is the ultimate luxury food for Torajans and they could not get enough of it. Chicken pie was the least offensive English food. The pie is a very English idea, difficult even in other European languages. Johannis referred to it as 'chicken cake'.

Before the opening of the exhibition, it was important that the rice-barn should at least resemble something under construction rather than a mere heap of wood. The carvers set to work with a will. The materials had been brought over in the form of large beams of wood and bamboo tiles for the roof. There is a great snobbery in tiles amongst the Toraja. The Baruppu' builders sneered at valley builders who cut tiles with saws instead of slicing them the manly way, with powerful strokes of a machete. Tiles cut by saw, they insisted, would rapidly rot. They began by constructing the central box of the barn – the part that would stand on the legs and that the roof would go on top of. It is a wonderful thing to see a Torajan carpenter mark a line on a thick tree trunk and convert it with a whir of machete strokes into a plank. The Torajans watched power tools at work and decided that, for most purposes, their own techniques were faster.

Once the box was complete, it would be disassembled, painted black, carved and coloured and rebuilt in its final position on top of the legs. Until then it made a handy changing room since they had to work with bare feet. Feet are as essential as hands for carving. They are used for gripping and steadying the wood that is being worked on. The gallery was rapidly converted into a convincing building site, knee-deep in wood shavings, teapots and cups.

There have been many efforts in recent years to liven up our museums, to convert them from the frosty banks of the art world into enjoyable and informative places. The great enemy of such moves is the glass case. Indispensable in its way, it nevertheless cuts off and insulates objects, makes them dead. Every museum curator knows that the exhibition everyone wants to get into is the one that he is trying to keep them out of, because it is still being built. Just as rehearsals are usually much more interesting than performances, so an exhibition in the course of arrangement offers much greater entertainment than the polished final product. The building site has an inherent fascination for the British: viewing platforms are provided on many construction sites so that the public can enjoy the spectacle. If one puts all this together, the Torajan exhibition seems inevitable.

The Torajans rapidly became used to the fact of people

watching them work and quite quickly 'regulars' became apparent – those who would come in several times a week to chart their progress. From the very first, Nenek loved it. In his own culture he is very much a star, a performer, and aware of the dignity of his position. Yet even at the beginning problems appeared.

The other carvers were all related to Nenek. The precise kinship had been collapsed and simplified. Any attempt to unravel them was greeted with, 'We are one family.' Because of his age and status as a priest, however, he expected great respect. Tanduk and Karre had been his pupils. Nowadays they worked as independent builders, but they had come together for the purposes of this exhibition. Nenek regarded them as his students, returned to work under his supervision. They had other views.

The first problem came, as in the theatre, with the billing. Around the rice-barn site were a number of panels explaining the enterprise and showing early stages of the collection of raw materials in Indonesia. Karre counted that Nenek appeared more often than himself. Nenek had even made the transition to the main background photographic display in his high priest's outfit. Tanduk too could be seen there in a shot of the market. Why had he been excluded? He appeared only slightly mollified when I pointed out the frequency with which his children appeared. Most of the children in the village seemed to be Karre's.

At later stages, Nenek insisted on demonstrating his authority, recutting a part that Karre had already worked. The dispute concerned whether a 'horn' – a sticking-out spur of the barn – should be straight or curved. From such problems, feuds begin. A cold war broke out. It began to look as if Karre and Nenek would not speak to each other again, that there would be an unfriendly atmosphere in the gallery. Fortunately, Third World people are hopelessly romanticized in our culture. One reviewer, visiting the museum, commented on the wonderful spirit of co-operation that enabled these people to work together without the need to exchange a word and expressed the hope that such might become the case in the British workplace.

British working practices were hard to understand. In Torajaland builders would labour from dawn to dusk until the job was done. Precise calculation of materials was never necessary. There was always more growing just up the hill. Normally, builders would sleep under the barn they were building, wrapped in their cloaks. They could not understand why this should not be so in England. It was impossible to get them to stop at 5 p.m. At that hour, it was still light in England. Indeed, unlike Indonesia where dusk is about six o'clock regardless of the season, it would continue to be light until much later. Why then should they lay down tools?

Sundays off they could understand. That was for going to church if you were Christian – or, in England, watching church services on television, which was even better. But not to work on Saturdays was monstrous. They rose, of course, as soon as it was light and expected all English people to be already at work as they would be back home.

The rice-barn grew little by little, and then in great leaps as the prepared sections were slotted together. Karre proved to be a relentless carving machine, churning out panel after panel of geometric forms. To his annoyance, however, only Nenek could produce the really complicated non-symmetrical patterns of gentle curves for the main beams. Nenek increased his discomfort by chewing areca-nut compulsively, in the knowledge that Karre was a smoker not allowed to smoke in the gallery. Visitors, too, clearly found Nenek a much more sympathetic carver than Karre. Being less concerned with speed, he was always willing to smile or call Johannis over to interpret so he could talk to people. Johannis, too, clearly enjoyed himself surprising visitors with his English and teaching young ladies how to paint.

When they returned to the house in the evening, the carvers would bath and eat, chat, watch television. They greatly appreciated a glass of beer – so hard to come by in Baruppu'. Nenek took a daily spoonful of the 'medicine' he had come to like. He had rapidly convinced all the museum guards that 'medicine' would make an appropriate present and began laying down a cellar.

But soon they would return to carving. Nenek erected a little bamboo table outside in the garden. When the weather was fine enough, he would carve out there. It had a strange, Robinson Crusoe appearance, with an umbrella tied on as sunshade. Johannis had been disparaging about the garden.

'You should plant all the flowers in straight lines, otherwise it is like the jungle.'

Nenek disagreed. 'This is a good garden. I have planted some coffee. I am sure it will grow here.'

He changed the subject. 'How much does a house like this cost?' I told him.

'Surely that cannot be right?' We did the calculations again. It was correct.

Nenek stared aghast. 'Have you *that* much money?' I explained about thirty-five-year mortgages and interest. He laughed. 'And Dutchmen keep coming and telling us we are crazy to spend all our money on buffalo to kill. You are the same with your houses. Houses are important to us too but we would never spend *that* much. Get me the wood and I will build you one for much less.'

'It is different here, Nenek,' explained Johannis with his worldly wisdom. 'Here, they do not have to pay school fees.' His obsession again.

Nenek indicated a man working on his house two or three doors down.

'Who is that man?'

'I don't know, Nenek. He just lives there.'

'You do not know his name?'

'No.'

'He is not one of your family?'

'No.'

He laid down his knife and looked at me in silent awe. 'Truly, you must be very strong to live so alone.'

The others colonized the kitchen, carving, painting, sharpening knives. We cooked rice in an artisanal workshop.

Much that we would have considered as waste, they employed for useful purposes. Plastic waterpipes left over from plumbing work were made into new handles for their knives. Old slates from the roof were speedily converted into fine whetstones. Nenek found an empty champagne bottle in a skip somewhere and used it for pounding clay to make earth colours, like a poignant symbol of the wastefulness of our culture. The plastic food trays from the plane were obviously far too valuable to throw away and he had surreptitiously removed them. They were now used as containers for paint.

He had a deep love of children. Frequently he would carve little panels depicting buffaloes and give them to children who came in to watch him. Often parents and teachers were so touched by this unexpected gesture that they went away in tears. Torajans were maintaining their reputation as great promoters of crying.

Problems with Indonesian 'butterflies' did not end in Surabaya and Ujung Pandang. The most popular brand of pressurized oil-lamp is also a 'butterfly' in Indonesia. To go into an ironmonger's shop and ask the Chinese girl behind the counter for a 'butterfly', however, involves no risk of misunderstanding. She will simply ask, *'Asli atau biasa?'* 'Do you want a genuine one or the normal sort?' It is a question that pulls you up short. In Indonesia, copyright laws are rudimentary. Most things are regularly copied, down to the trademark. Copies are often just as good as the original but they are expected to be cheaper.

The question could also be asked of the rice-barn the carvers were building. In their native village of Baruppu', rice-barns do not normally have bamboo roofs. Roofs are generally of wooden slates or the inner bark of a particular palm-tree, a material rather like a Brillo pad. If you ask why this should be so, Baruppu'ans will explain that there was a terrible fire some thirty years ago that destroyed all suitable bamboo for roofs. If bamboo tiles were to be used, they would have to be imported at huge cost from the valley. Only a rich man could conceive of such a notion. If you point to the magnificent stands of bamboo around the village that were the undoing of Johannis's cousin, they say that they cannot be sure but, in all probability, this bamboo is not suitable for roofs. Since bamboo roofs should last up to fifty years and the fire was thirty years ago, the arithmetic does not quite add up. The fact seems to be that, while everyone knows that – ideally – a barn should have a bamboo roof, no one can or wants to spend the money on one.

When it came to discussions about the museum rice-barn, the Torajans were horrified at the suggestion that a barn in *a museum* should have anything other than a bamboo roof. It would, they explained laughing, be crude, improper. They would be ashamed. If people came from Indonesia, they would be ridiculed. So the barn in the museum had to have a fine bamboo roof of a type that they had had in their heads since they were children but rarely built. I am not sure whether this made it *more* or *less* genuine. This was, it seemed, the reason that Karre had been selected. He was the one man in Baruppu' who had done a bamboo roof before. A certain lack of experience was revealed, however, in his estimates of the time and material needed for the job. One day he would announce that the roof would take two months. There was only half the material needed. The next day it would take only three weeks. There would be plenty of bamboo left over. On really bad days the carvers would have long discussions about the roof and then troop up to my office to look at a photograph of a rice-barn, turning it gloomily this way and that. It was all very unnerving, since there was absolutely no possibility of securing more bamboo in England at so late a stage.

While the public enjoyed the spectacle of the rice-barn, it was a fine opportunity to document the entire process of its construction and collect information that would be very difficult to acquire in the field. It became more and more evident how great is the cultural importance of the rice-barn.

In form it is like a Torajan house except that it normally faces south rather than north. It is much more than merely a place to store food. It is also important for the spirits that control the fertility of the rice.

In anthropology the Torajans are known as the standard example of a form of classification termed 'complementary binary opposition'. Such a complex name masks a very simple principle. The entire world is divided up into opposites, such as light/dark, right/left, male/female, life/death, which govern appropriate behaviour. In theory, then, it is possible simply to read off the essential elements of any Torajan ceremony in terms of these opposites. If one is present at a festival of life, it will be morning, people will be facing east, wearing light clothes and so on. If it is a festival of death it will be past noon, people will be facing west, clad in black, etc., etc. Such classifications can be seen to be active in the most minor and seemingly irrational acts – a hidden structure lying behind the apparent chaos of another culture. Unfortunately, it never quite seems to work.

The rice-barn, as stated, is like a house but all the directions are reversed. This is particularly clear when guests of honour are required to sit on the platform of the barn. Instead of sitting at the north-east, the normally auspicious side, they sit at the south-west, usually associated with death. In this way, normal spatial patterns are reversed within the rice-barn. That this is so might seem odd but it can be accounted for as part of a wider phenomenon of inversion and mediation. Thus, mediators – things that belong neither to one firm category nor another – are often inverted. The standard example in our own culture is the point where the old year joins the new. New Year festivals are characterized by army officers waiting on their men and all sorts of absurdities of dress and behaviour.

Torajan rites rigorously segregate and oppose the ceremonies of the east and west, those of life and death. The only point at which these meet – are mediated – is the rice-barn. It is here that the seed for next year's crop is kept. Here too, in the days when Torajans were headhunters, human skulls were stored to increase general fertility and well-being; the point, then, at which life and death meet and are converted into each other.

In many areas it is the moment at which a corpse is placed on the rice-barn that marks the official start of death. Until then, the (to us) deceased is spoken of as 'having a headache'. In Baruppu' they do not do this, but have a further refinement. The word for a rice-barn is *alang*. The bier on which the dead body is transported to the tomb is made in the form of a rice-barn but of throwaway materials – paper and plywood. It is called an *alang-alang*. The rice-barn then is the device that shunts people from one ritual position to another. The reversal of directions is appropriate.

Yet this explanation too seems inadequate. Nenek gave me a lot of information about festivals and rice-barns while working in the museum, but it was interesting that while the geographical directions involved were always 'correct', he constantly changed the reasons why they were so. Why did an honoured guest sit in the inauspicious south-west of the barn? Because the barn faced south not north so directions were changed. Was that why a priest of life sat on the west side? No, he did so so that he could face east, the auspicious side. The more one tried to tie up abstract classifications with what people actually did, the clearer it became that the system was unbreachable. You could always find a reason for justifying what people did even if that reason contradicted one invoked earlier. So the classifications were not the rules of iron that they appeared to be to the outsider. They were merely something to be nodded towards deferentially.

The carving on a barn is the same as that on the house. Each of the motifs has a name, and the position that it can occupy on the barn is subject to rules. For example, the motif of cockerels standing on sunbursts should go high under the eaves. It simultaneously combines many meanings as do the other motifs. Whole books have been written on the patterns of Torajan carving.

During the construction process, however, a further point emerged. I had climbed on to the barn to take some pictures of the technique by which roof-tiles are attached and was joking with the carvers. There was a sudden cry of rage from Nenek down below.

'Stop that!' he shouted. 'You must never joke on a rice-barn.' What could he mean? 'The house is the mother,' he explained, 'the rice-barn is the father.' Binary opposition again. 'When you are building a house, you can gossip and play about, it does not matter. But a rice-barn is a male thing, it is serious. Mice are playful animals. If you joke while building a rice-barn, they will invade it and gobble up the rice.'

Torajan religion makes much use of the killing of animals. Nenek was keen that the rice-barn should be completed with due ceremony. In Torajaland that would normally involve the killing of a pig and the pronouncement of a blessing by Nenek. There were all sorts of reasons – legal, moral, sanitational – why this would be awkward to organize inside a public museum. Nenek was understanding but regretful.

'It is not right. It is not' – he had learned the power of the word in an ethnographic museum – 'traditional.'

We mulled over the possibility of buying a side of pork. Nenek dismissed it.

'A rice-barn,' he asserted dramatically, 'needs blood.' It was to get some.

I was up on the roof, talking – but not joking – with the carvers.

'Pass me that machete,' said Tanduk, 'the one stuck in that bamboo beam.'

I reached out and grabbed the bamboo, not realizing that the blade projected through the other side. Torajans keep their cutting implements honed to a razor-sharp perfection. Indeed, the carvers used to shave with their carving knives. The machete sliced clean through a finger, severing the artery. A pulsing spurt of blood shot out over the apex of the roof. As I rushed away in search of first aid, a small, slightly triumphant voice called after me, 'We won't have to kill that pig now.'

Of all the carvers, Nenek was by far the most adventurous. Indonesians have a ready-made response to questions about why they suddenly changed the habits of a lifetime and did something completely new. All such actions can be explained by *cari pengalaman*, 'to seek experience', which is unquestioningly regarded as good. Nenek was gripped by this urge to discover. If there was a high building around or a hill to climb, Nenek would want to do it. If there was something new to eat or drink, Nenek would go first.

'He is too old. Leave him at home,' Johannis would say with the heartlessness of the young. But Nenek refused to be left.

Every morning, when I crept blearily downstairs, he would be sitting in the kitchen carving contentedly until I made him a cup of tea. (Only later did I learn that drinking coffee is forbidden for a Torajan priest.) On the second morning he surprised me. 'Mercowe,' he said. I didn't understand. It sounded like a sea monster from *Beowulf*. It must be Torajan. I would have to ask Johannis.

'Mercowe,' he insisted, looking at me.

'I don't understand, Nenek.' He grabbed me by the hand and led me to the front door. The *welcome* mat was upside down and back to front. It read, *mercowe*. He had begun to learn English.

He adored looking at strange animals. 'Strange' included many Indonesian animals he had never seen before. The greatest success was, without doubt, the zoo. The Torajans jumped up and down with delight at the sight of orang utans. They were suitably repelled by snakes, getting from them the titillating *frisson* that we get from a horror film. A wicked child terrified Nenek with a rubber snake in the reptile house. When he realized his mistake he laughed at it for days. 'I like it when people play tricks.' Nenek loved the gorilla. 'Wah! Are you sure it cannot reach us?' The giraffe was so strange an idea that he initially refused to accept it as natural. 'Was it born like that? Does it eat people?' As usual, it was not the animals you would have expected that commanded most attention. Buffalo and bison, for all their centrality to Torajan life, were dismissed. Far more interesting were horses – an English horse is two or three times the size of a Torajan horse – and, above all, dogs.

Torajans have a relatively kindly approach to dogs. They eat them but also pet them and talk to them. Most Torajan dogs are the runty, prick-eared creatures standard throughout South East

Asia, but Dutch influence has added absurdly fluffy specimens that are much admired. The sheer variety of English dogs, the way they were allowed a free run of the house surprised them. Most extraordinary was their encounter with a Great Dane. 'Is that a *dog?*' Indeed, it was almost as large as a Torajan horse. They were terrified initially but were rapidly won over by its good nature. Within five minutes Nenek was stroking it – but in such a way that you felt he was pondering the problem of how best to slice it at the joints.

Yet it was not this that struck them the most. One day they arrived back in great hilarity.

'The park,' they said, 'is full of madmen.' Oh dear.

'What did they do?'

They giggled. 'They walked round ... with dogs ... on the ends of pieces of string.' Again they fell around with laughter.

'But you do the same with buffaloes. You take them for swims. I have seen people oiling their hooves and brushing their eyelashes.'

Of course, they agreed huffily. But that was different. To do that with a dog was like doing it with a mouse. Crazy!

In the second month of their stay, the weather improved long enough for them to visit some of the sights of the city. Ancient buildings of stone left them cold. Even the Christians were unimpressed by the great age attributed to Westminster Abbey and other churches. The Tower of London, Greenwich, they found frankly boring. The most successful monument was Tower Bridge. I asked Johannis why. 'It is on calendars in Indonesia,' he explained. An unexpected second was the Foreign and Commonwealth Office. As I was leading them on a somewhat vague and undirected walk around central London, they happened to notice the carving around the door. It was a simple geometric pattern but very similar to one used as a filler on Torajan buildings. How had it got there? Had it been stolen from the Torajans? They were all for rushing up and asking the Minister at once.

We went on a day trip to Oxford, an extremely unfriendly and unwelcoming place to the visitor. Most sites of interest were firmly shut against them. As usual, it proved difficult to gain admission to a pub in order to get out of the rain, and everyone in the catering trade was astonished at people wanting to eat on a Sunday. The trip was redeemed by one incident only. The carvers were unused to having to master their bladders. In Torajaland, after all, one can urinate anywhere. We were constantly obliged to make emergency stops. One of these on the way home happened to involve urinating at the back of my former school. It was thought-provoking how many coincidences and unlikely events had had to occur so that I could visit it in such circumstances with a group of Indonesian hill tribesmen.

Like Japanese tourists, when they found anything impressive they never simply photographed it, but required a group portrait standing in front of and almost wholly obscuring it. Time and again they appear clenched together with cheesy smiles in front of famous places. Even Nenek and Karre would smile fraternally for the camera until a shot was over and they could resume mutual scowls.

'It is like photographing the cat together with the mouse,' said Johannis delightedly.

After some two months, the rice-barn was looking more and more convincing. The carvers had stretched it to fit the gallery exactly, something that increased my unease about the supplies of building materials. As the roof progressed, the construction turned into an aerial display. A large wooden scaffolding had been erected all round the barn and on this they swung and balanced as the tiles were threaded on splints of rattan and tied down layer by layer. The characteristic curve of the roof was achieved by attaching a stout rope between the central beam and a major floor beam and simply twisting a stick through until sufficient pressure was exerted to give the correct shape.

Although Johannis had been brought primarily as a link, he showed himself more and more active in the process of construction. While from a carving family, he had never practised such skills, opting for a modern model whereby a man progresses in the world through school and university. His attitude to Nenek was therefore ambivalent. He was a reminder of Johannis's rustic origins, therefore an embarrassment. Yet he swiftly perceived that Nenek was, if anything, accorded more respect in England than in Torajaland. He was astonished at the interest and admiration shown his carving skills and the obvious attractiveness of his personality. He and Nenek began to have whispered conversations at night. One day, grinning with bashfulness, he picked up a piece of wood and started to carve. The other younger men immediately hooted in derision but Johannis smiled and quietly persevered. His natural talent was immediately obvious. It was a more than competent rendition of a traditional motif. He puffed out his chest with pride and promptly sold it to the Indonesian restaurant where he went to collect their midday food. After that he never looked back. He could produce a geometric design at the drop of a hat. He began innovating. 'This is a traditional design but I have turned these lines into transistors like in my brother's electronic circuit drawings.' Within days he had graduated from merely painting the carvings of others to working on the barn in his own right. In the evenings the kitchen was even more congested. There was another carver in the house.

When not carving, they would watch television compulsively, harassing Johannis to translate for them until he could stand it no longer. War was extremely popular, followed by sex. Love scenes did not have to sink very deep to be considered highly pornographic, since censorship in Indonesia is strict in such matters. A sure sign that a programme was being enjoyed was to hear them tutting in disapproval. Most popular of all, of course, were advertisements, now discontinued on Indonesian television, and I would hear them humming the tunes in the bathroom, interspersed with the patriotic ditties that feature so largely in their own country. Sometimes they sang patriotic words to the jingles advertising chewing gum and lavatory paper.

Their standards of criticism were harsh, however. Their view of the Open University programmes was, 'There was too much story, not enough women and no one got shot.' Nenek alone seemed to enjoy programmes of intellectual content. He watched a whole course on quantum physics with evident enjoyment and thoroughly savoured a biography of the late Ernest Hemingway, breaking off to comment, 'It's good to see people who are old like me.'

It was on his trips to the restaurant in Soho that Johannis discovered the seamier side of London life. He must have passed this knowledge on to Karre because the latter began to inquire on the activities of 'hontesses' (their version of 'hostesses'). When informed of probable prices, however, he was scandalized.

'I could get a buffalo for that – quite a pretty one.'

At the time AIDS was widely, if briefly, advertised on television, to the point that one of the carvers was convinced he had mysteriously caught it. Fortunately, it turned out to be dandruff.

All parents know that sudden realization that the house is just too quiet. The children must be up to something – and something wicked. It shows how far I had unwittingly slipped into the parental role that I had exactly that reaction one evening. I crept into the doorway. From the living-room came sounds of tutting and tittering. Exercising that ingenuity for which Torajans deserve to be famed, they had come to a deal with the waiters at the Indonesian restaurant – carvings for videos, art for porn.

Relations between Nenek and Karre continued frosty, Tanduk sometimes exercising a moderating influence, sometimes supporting Karre. Johannis won a great deal of my respect for the way he dampened down conflict. They quickly adapted their style of disagreement to the possibilities of an English house. Karre was the first to discover the dramatic possibilities of stairs. They were ideal for stalking up in outrage with a final insult tossed over one shoulder. Nenek, however, discovered door-slamming. Torajan doors are small and tend not to have a knob that allows them to be slammed without trapping your fingers. Unfortunately, several of the doors in my house were not ideal for slamming with force because the carpet prevented it. The only good slam in the house was the bathroom door but you were then obliged to sulk in there until driven out by boredom.

If Johannis acted as a moderating influence in domestic Torajan affairs, he none the less enjoyed teasing me. He let slip the information that Karre had been in trouble for violence against another man in the village.

'But that,' he said sweetly, 'was an affair of buffalo and women. It could happen to anyone.'

Karre launched into a new offensive by moving into Nenek's sphere. He began to offer explanations and interpretations of the patterns he carved. While Nenek 'explained' in terms of names of motifs and general principles like 'riches' or 'luck' that they represented, Karre offered proverbs. When marking out the motif conventionally glossed as 'tadpoles', for example, he declared in front of Nenek. 'We put these on a barn to show that many should live together and each respect the other like tadpoles in a rice-field. No one tries to be chief.'

He also added a new twist to the interpretation of the cockerels carved on the eaves: 'We put them here to show how men should *not* behave – like animals that put themselves above others.'

In his own way Karre was making the point that the traditional motifs of Torajan life can be adapted to the demands of a new morality. Like the apparently rigid binary oppositions of Torajan classification, they could be used in infinitely flexible ways.

As it turned out, there was no shortage of material for the rice-barn roof. The structure was finished in good time and we were able to have a formal completion ceremony at which Nenek, to the rage of Karre, pronounced a blessing but no pigs were killed.

Relations between them had further declined when Nenek completed the barn by carving his own name in large letters on the door. Karre got up specially early and obliterated the name. Nenek was very calm.

'He is a man of no culture,' he declared loftily, pleased, I suspect, that this action had proved his assessment of his former pupil. He took me to one side.

'Wait till we have gone home, then paint my name back in.'

There now came the moment I had been dreading – payment.

The original contract had been negotiated in buffalo but there is a recognized rate for converting buffalo into money. The young carvers had decided they wanted money and Nenek had gone along with this. This was surprising. The problem with cash is that it can be seized by rapacious relatives and divided up infinitely while a buffalo is indivisible. The problem now was whether we should pay everyone the same amount or whether Nenek as the head should receive more. The younger carvers had insisted that all should receive the same. Half-way through the operation, I suddenly saw myself as they must be seeing me. I had a vision of a little old man up on a bamboo platform at the end of a funeral. He was distributing meat, calling out the names and flinging down portions of dead buffalo. It is the moment when people's standing and rank are publicly declared and fixed for years to come, a time of strong passions and prickly sensibilities, when resentments rise to the surface and fights break out. Already Nenek was bristling with outrage, ready to leap to his feet. Karre had his arms crossed truculently. Even mild Tanduk glowered. Only Johannis grinned his enjoyment of others' discomfort. This was clearly a situation where a beginner was going to do himself no good. There were awkward moments before a satisfactory solution was reached whereby all apparently received the same *payment* while Nenek received an additional *present*. Even more important was that the others should know that he had received extra money but not know how much.

'What will you do with this money, Nenek?'

His eyes twinkled. 'I shall save it. Save it for my old age.'

To enter into an agreement such as this, with people from a culture very unlike our own, was fraught with problems of a moral kind. It is a moral space, indeed, from which *all* exits are shut off in advance.

Ethnographic exhibitions involving people are not new. In the nineteenth century they were common. One offered as its chief attraction the chance of seeing a savage Filipino eat a dead dog.

Participants can have had little knowledge of what lay in store for them and were treated like wild animals in a zoo. At the end of the exhibition, they were sometimes simply thrown out to fend for themselves.

The world has changed since then but power relations are still very unequal. It is hard to protect people in a world they do not understand without being accused of paternalism, or leave them scope for initiative without being accused of neglect. To treat them as one would Englishmen is cultural imperialism, to insist upon their difference from us smacks of racism. To ask members of another culture to 'perform' seems demeaning, while to ask our own artists to do so is not. It was clear, however, that the Torajans did not feel humiliated but honoured. They were not dressing up in tribal costume to do something just for tourists. As far as the carvers were concerned, this was another contract for another rice-barn. They returned to their own culture with increased status and wealth. Johannis's parents had been firm.

'We would not let him go if we did not know you and trust you. He wants to go. It will be good for him.'

It is good to be able to organize an exhibition that does not simply take from a Third World country but fosters a skill under threat. In a sense, the best tribute was that Johannis, a thoroughly modern Torajan, started carving. In a sense it seemed as if it was through coming to London that he had fully become a Torajan. It was, however, with mixed feelings that I listened as he explained to me that now he had enough money to go to university, he would have to write a thesis. He had decided, having watched me work, that he would turn his grandfather into his thesis. He was well on the way to making that divide between traditional and modern life that characterizes the former as 'custom' – a party hat, or in this case an academic cap, to be lightly put on and off at will.

What did they make of us? It is perhaps easier to get at an answer than might be thought. Torajans have a refreshing directness. For example, once I gave Johannis a shirt, for which he thanked me. When I asked him if he liked it, however, he said no, quite frankly he did not. Torajans often seem to tell the truth when we would tell small lies simply to be polite.

When it was time to go home, two were homesick and two were not. Johannis said that he had enjoyed his time here but he looked forward to returning home. Tanduk was desperate to go home and plant his fields. He explained that he had seven children, which was why he wanted to go back. Karre, on the other hand, had eight, which was why he wanted to stay. Were there not other people here who wanted a rice-barn? He would gladly build one. Most surprising, it was Nenek who was keenest to stay. 'The food is good here. English people are nicer. Why should I want to go back? I have planted coffee in your garden. I want to harvest it.'

One critic remarked that it was all very well to bring such people here and treat them kindly, but doing this would only make them unhappy when they went back home. That is an argument for never trying to be nice to anyone. Only one incident raised doubts about the effect on the Torajans.

Anthropology largely neglects the individual to deal in generalizations. Generalizations always tell a little lie in the service of a greater truth. Yet I was increasingly aware that I had brought over four Torajans but would be sending them back as four individuals. They were no longer simply carriers of a particular culture but real people. As is the Indonesian way, I bought them all a present before they left, something to remember me by. For most, it was obvious what to get. There were things they had seen and admired. But Karre was a problem. Was there not, I asked, something that he would like that he might not be able to get in Baruppu'? Yes, he said. Now that he had all this money, he would like a strong lock for his door because other people would want to steal it.

Airports are bad places for farewells. The carvers were to be met in Jakarta and looked after by some fellow Torajans, but with their luggage stacked about them, wearing shoes, they looked like refugees. As was to be expected, they all burst into tears and sobbed whole-heartedly. I remembered the time on that wind-swept plateau when Torajans had extended to me the sign of common humanity, the offer to cry with them. I did not refuse it now either.

'Write me a letter,' said Nenek. 'Johannis can read it to me.'

Four of my handkerchiefs disappeared through the barrier with them. As they were about to disappear, there was a sudden shrilling of alarm bells and a stamping rush of security men. I had reminded them that they could not carry knives and swords in their hand luggage. I had not realized they had put them in their pockets and worn them round their waists.

Johannis looked embarrassed and laughed, the others looked worried. No one would let me through the barrier. There was nothing I could do. They were already on their way back to their own world. There was a deal of heavy-footed head-shaking, a scratching of chins by men in uniforms. Finally, the 'weapons' were retained and they were led off to the plane. Johannis turned and gave a final laugh. Nenek was too short to see over the barrier but I heard a voice call, 'Don't forget to harvest the coffee.'

Also by Nigel Barley,

published by Monsoon Books

IN THE FOOTSTEPS OF
STAMFORD RAFFLES

Nigel Barley

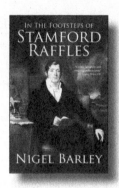

Stamford Raffles is that rarest of things — a colonial figure who is forgotten at home but still remembered with affection abroad. Born into genteel poverty in 1781, he joined the East India Company at the age of fourteen and worked his way up to become Lieutenant Governor of Java when the British seized that island for some five years in 1811. There he fell in love with all things Javanese and vaunted it as a place of civilization as he discovered himself as a man of science as well as commerce. A humane and ever-curious figure, his administration was a period of energetic reform and boisterous research that culminated in his History of Java in 1817 and it remains the starting-point of all subsequent studies of Indonesian culture.

Personal tragedy and ill-health stalked his final years in the East. Yet, though dying at the early age of 44 and dogged by the hostility of lesser men, he would still find time to found the city-state of Singapore and guide it through its first dangerous years. Here, mythologised by the British and demonised by the Dutch, he is more than a remote founding father and remains a charter for its independence and its enduring values.

In this intriguing book, part history, part travelogue, Nigel Barley re-visits the places that were important in the life of Stamford Raffles and evaluates his heritage in an account that is both humorous and insightful.

ROGUE RAIDER

The Tale of Captain Lauterbach,
the Singapore Mutiny and the audacious
Battle of Penang

NIGEL BARLEY

It is the First World War and the Flashmanesque
German naval reserve captain, Julius Lauterbach,
is a prisoner of war in the old Tanglin barracks of Singapore. He is also
a braggart, a womaniser and a heavy drinker and through his bored
fantasies he unwittingly triggers a mutiny by Muslim troops of the
British garrison — the 1915 Singapore Mutiny — and so throws the
whole course of the war in doubt. The British lose control of the city, its
European inhabitants flee to the ships in the harbour and it is only with
the help of Japanese marines that the Empire is saved.

Rogue Raider is the adventure story of how one ship, the *Emden*,
ties up the navies of four nations and audaciously starts the Battle of
Penang in Malaysia, and how one man eludes Allied Forces in a desperate
chase across Indonesia and the rest of Asia to America as he attempts to
regain his native land.

It is fictionalised history but a true history that was deliberately
suppressed by the British authorities of the time as too embarrassing
and dangerous to be known. Revealed here, it brings vividly to life the
Southeast Asia of the period, its sights, its sounds and its rich mix of
peoples. And through it an unwilling participant in the war becomes an
accidental hero.

ISLAND OF DEMONS

NIGEL BARLEY

Many men dream of running away to a tropical island and living surrounded by beauty and exotic exuberance. Walter Spies did more than dream. He actually did it.

In the 1920s and 30s, Walter Spies — ethnographer, choreographer, film maker, natural historian and painter — transformed the perception of Bali from that of a remote island to become the site for Western fantasies about Paradise and it underwent an influx of foreign visitors. The rich and famous flocked to Spies' house in Ubud and his life and work forged a link between serious academics and the visionaries from the Golden Age of Hollywood. Charlie Chaplin, Noel Coward, Miguel Covarrubias, Vicki Baum, Barbara Hutton and many others sought to experience the vision Spies offered while Margaret Mead and Gregory Bateson, the foremost anthropologists of their day, attempted to capture the secret of this tantalizing and enigmatic culture.

Island of Demons is a fascinating historical novel, mixing anthropology, the history of ideas and humour. It offers a unique insight into that complex and multi-hued world that was so soon to be swept away, exploring both its ideas and the larger than life characters that inhabited it.

SNOW OVER SURABAYA

Nigel Barley

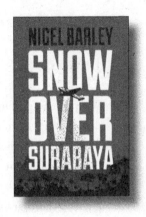

Not many Glaswegian schoolgirls have grown up to become revolutionary heroes of distant, eastern nations but Muriel Stewart Walker did just that.

Under a multitude of different names – 'K'tut Tantri' and 'Surabaya Sue' being the best known – this Scottish-born, self-proclaimed Hollywood scriptwriter joined in the struggle for Indonesian independence after the Second World War and broadcast its revolutionary message to the world on Rebel Radio. But she did more and smuggled arms, and probably drugs, to help finance the new Republic and experienced bloody battle in the November 1945 British attack on Surabaya that some have seen as a war crime. She went on to become an intimate of the revolutionary leaders, Bung Tomo and Soekarno among them, and finally lived to see Indonesia take its place amongst the free nations of the world.

Surabaya Sue is virtually unknown in the West and, even in Indonesia, there have always been doubts about her version of events that many have dismissed outright as a blatant mixture of outrageous fantasy and dishonest omissions. *Snow over Surabaya* happily embraces those doubts and brings a new, spirited account of her adventures in that tempestuous world.